# OUR CATS ARE PLOTTING TO KILL US

Jim Tilberry

*"The constant challenge to decipher feline behavior
is perhaps one of the most fascinating qualities
of owning a cat."*

Carole Wilbourn
The Cat Therapist

## Chapter 1

Julie Belcher had not slept well the night before and was feeling stressed. On her lunch break at Supercuts, she carried her sandwich and coffee to her car and called her twin sister.

Linda answered, "Hey Sis, what's up?"

"Last night I dreamed my cats buried me alive in a litter box."

"Had the box been scooped recently, or was it filled with smelly clumps? That would make a difference."

"I didn't notice any clumps around me, just the grainy litter. But it was still a terrifying dream. I was completely submerged, and the cats were standing next to the box laughing at me."

"That's wild. Is there something going on with you and the cats?"

Julie sipped her coffee. "Yes, in fact there is. This is going to sound weird, but they both regularly give me a look."

"What type of look?"

"An 'F-you' look."

Linda grimaced and shook her head. "That's silly. Dismissive looks are typical of a lot of cats, right? I mean they're not exactly known for their big, friendly smiles."

"I know. But the cats I've had before always seemed nicer and happier to see me. These cats seem kind of edgy. And I think they deliberately do things to piss me off."

"Like what?

"Well they often poop in the litter box the moment I'm done scooping it out. It's as if they're purposely holding it in just so they can soil the litter right after I cleaned it. Now why would they do that other than to irritate me?"

"That might be annoying, but cats can't possibly be that deliberate. They're *cats*. That's got to be a coincidence."

Julie bit into her sandwich and mustard dripped down her chin. After wiping her face, she looked back at Linda. "When I was typing on my laptop, Oliver squatted on the keyboard, blocking my view of the screen."

"Aww. Cute."

"Then he peed."

"Oh."

"Doused the keyboard and my pants."

"Well that sounds like an attempt to get attention."

"And when I was sleeping, Wendell jumped on the bed and bit my shoulder."

"Like a gentle nibble to wake you up?"

Julie held up her open hand with fingers apart. "I needed five stitches."

"Ouch."

"Ever since we adopted our cats and the dog at the shelter three months ago, I've been a bit frazzled. The cats are pissed at me, and I wish I knew why."

"What does Darryl think?"

"Darryl is clueless. He thinks the cats are fine and that I'm just imagining they don't like me. And maybe he's right. I don't know."

Linda perked up. "There's a way to find out."

"How?"

"Remember when I told you about the animal communicator I used?"

"Do you think she could find out what the cats are thinking?"

"No doubt. She's helped me a lot with understanding Bailey's late-night barking."

"What'd she say?"

"Nightmares. He dreams that cats rule the world."

"I think he's right, Linda. But I know Darryl would not want to spend money on an animal psychic. He doesn't believe any psychics are legit."

Linda nodded and smiled. "Let me just talk to Patricia. We've become friends, and maybe she'll give you a deal."

"Great and thanks. I'd like to know if I'm just imagining this stuff or if, as I suspect, the cats really do hate my guts."

"Try to think positive. Even if Oliver and Wendell do bury you in cat litter, it might not kill you. And even if it did, think of your interesting obituary: 'Woman buried alive in litter box by her own cats.'"

## Chapter 2

Patricia Van Winkle didn't mince words with Julie. "Your cats hate you. Apparently, you and Darryl do a lot of stuff that pisses them off. I'm sorry, but your cats are *not* happy campers."

"Oh no, I was afraid of that. What did they tell you?"

"In my psychic communications, they mentioned a few things that led me to this conclusion. First, there are too many closed doors in your house, like the closets, bedrooms, and basement. They're frustrated because they can't enter these areas and explore."

Julie pulled out a pen and notepad, scribbled a few words, and said, "Closed doors doesn't sound like enough of a reason to hate us. What else is bothering them?"

"They don't like being shooed off the kitchen counter. They enjoy climbing up there and resent being made to get off."

"Still doesn't seem like a reason to hate us. What else have we done?"

"Oliver said you spilled gravy all over him."

Julie jotted down some notes. "That was an accident on Thanksgiving. I was carrying the gravy boat to the table and Oliver was underfoot, so I tripped over him." *I'm such a klutz.*

"He also resents being made the butt of jokes, like when your husband said, 'Oliver looks delicious. We should eat *him* instead of the turkey.'"

"Darryl just has a weird sense of humor. Wait, Oliver can understand us?" *Uh oh.*

"Yes, both cats understand everything you say."

"That can't be good. What else did they complain about?"

"Wendell claimed that Darryl threw up on him."

"Ugh. That was New Year's Eve when Darryl had way too many beers. Unfortunately, Wendell was just in the wrong place at the wrong time. I'm sure Darryl didn't mean to puke on him. What else?"

"Did you really pour a bucket of blue paint on Oliver a few weeks ago?"

Julie groaned. "Believe me, it wasn't deliberate. I was painting the office and the can fell off the ladder right onto Oliver's head. I suppose I should've closed the door."

"Oliver called you 'criminally negligent.'"

"Maybe, but it was very funny. He looked like a Smurf."

"Oliver felt ugly and humiliated."

Julie wrote, "Puke on Wendell, gravy and blue paint on Oliver." *We're terrible people.* "Is there anything else?"

"Well, yes. They have what sound like insulting nicknames for both of you."

"What? No, don't tell me. I'd rather not know."

Julie was distraught after hearing this disturbing news, but in her heart she knew it was true. The cats hated her and Darryl. She would have to share this troubling information with him.

\*\*\*\*\*

"The cats adore us. That psychic is full of crap," said Darryl as he rolled over on the couch and grabbed a handful of Doritos.

Julie frowned. "No, she's totally legit. Patricia Van Winkle is one of the foremost animal communicators around. She knows her stuff and was right about so much."

"Did she even *meet* Oliver and Wendell?"

"No, I told you how she works. I sent her a photo and she used that picture to tap into their psychic energy."

Darryl sat up and took a swig of beer. "What a bunch of hooey. You can't telepathically communicate with dumb animals. It's just not possible. She's a charlatan like all other scam-artist psychics."

"Then how would you explain the specific things she knew about both us and the cats?"

"Like what?"

"Well, she knew that we have closed doors in the house, and the cats don't like to be locked out of rooms and closets."

Darryl rolled his eyes. "That's news? I'm sure most cats aren't happy about closed doors. She really didn't need to go out on a limb to guess that."

"All right. How do you explain she knew that you threw up on Wendell?"

"Why would that make him hate us? *Cats* puke all the time. I'm sure he could relate. It was more of a bonding experience."

Julie shook her head and glanced at her notes. "Then explain how she knew I spilled a bucket of blue paint on Oliver."

"Lucky guess."

"You are in total denial. Our cats hate us, and we're making their lives miserable. We need to find out how we can make them like us again."

"That's ridiculous. Those cats have a great life. They get all the food they can eat and get to sleep all day. I would trade lives with them in a heartbeat."

"You're kidding? You would like be confined to this house all the time? I doubt it."

"Sleep 'til noon. Drink beer all day. Unlimited TV. What's not to like?"

Julie stared at Darryl. "You're a knucklehead."

"I'm a knucklehead? At least I'm not dumb enough to waste money on an 'animal communicator,'" he said, using air quotes. "By the way, how much did Rip-off Van Winkle cost?"

"Her name is *Patricia* Van Winkle. And because I was referred by Linda, she only charged me half price."

"Which was how much?"

"We can afford it. Don't worry."

"How much?"

"A hundred dollars."

"Holy crap. A hundred bucks to find out our cats don't like closed doors. Great investment. Yeah, *I'm* the knucklehead."

## Chapter 3

Julie nudged Darryl's shoulder and whispered, "Darryl, wake up. Wake up."

Darryl awkwardly swung his legs off the couch and planted them on the floor. "What? What's going on?"

"Shhhh. Keep your voice down."

"Why? What's happening?"

"You need to see something. Follow me upstairs, but be very quiet."

"Is there someone in the house?"

"Shhhh... no. Please be quiet."

Julie tiptoed up the stairs and led Darryl to the guest bedroom. They stood by the door, which was partially closed. Julie pointed to the two cats who were on the bed facing each other and whispered, "Look."

"I can't believe you woke me up to look at the stupid cats."

"Be quiet and pay attention. Look what they're doing."

Oliver looked at Wendell as he nodded his head. Then Wendell stared back and Oliver nodded several times. They went back and forth until Wendell caught sight of Julie and Darryl. Both cats hopped off the bed and strutted out of the room, passing in front of their owners.

Julie turned toward Darryl. "What do you think about that?"

"What?"

"You just saw them with your own eyes. They were silently communicating."

"No, they weren't. They were just looking at each other, which doesn't mean a thing."

"They were having a nonverbal conversation, and as soon as they saw us eavesdropping, they stopped talking."

"Eh... I don't know. That sounds pretty farfetched."

"Darryl, they were speaking to each other telepathically."

"Okay, so maybe they were reading each other's minds. What do you want me to do about it?"

"You heard what the animal psychic said about the cats, how they probably hate us. Maybe I should have Patricia do another session with them. We need to find out what they're thinking."

Darryl shook his head. "And flush another hundred bucks down the toilet? No way."

"Then what would *you* suggest we do?"

"Why do we have to do anything? What's the big deal?"

Julie's voice cracked in frustration. "What's the big deal? They're probably 'talking' about us, and it's probably not good. We need to find out what they're thinking and what we should be doing differently."

"You are just obsessed with these stupid cats. All right, let me think about. But don't hire that lady yet. Maybe there's a cheaper way." *Or better yet, you'll just forget about all this goofy nonsense.*

## Chapter 4

That evening Julie came into the family room and said, "I've got it! I found a way to learn what the cats say to each other, and it probably won't cost us anything. All we need to do is secretly record their brain waves."

Darryl looked away from the basketball game on TV and toward his wife. "Oh, is *that* all we have to do?"

"Yes."

Darryl gawked at Julie for a couple of seconds. "Have you totally lost your mind? First, I'm fairly certain cats don't even have brains. But assuming they did, how would we even do that?"

"I found an app called 'Cat Chat' that translates cats' thoughts into English. It was created specifically for people who own more than one cat."

Darryl hit the mute button for the TV. "For real?"

"Yes, I did a Google search for 'How to translate your cat's thoughts,' and it was the first listing. The app was created by Elon Musk in his spare time."

"Elon Musk has spare time?"

"Apparently so. He created it to find out if his two cats would like to fly to Mars."

"That's insane. Cats freak out on short car rides. Why would he think they'd want to ride a rocket ship for six months?"

"Maybe his cats are different. I mean, Musk is definitely different."

"You mean definitely kooky. Do you think this app really works?"

"Of course it works... probably."

Darryl tossed his hands in the air. "Ugh. You're making too much of what that phony psychic said. Our cats don't hate us. Can't you just let it go?"

Julie sat next to him and put her hand on his arm. "I can't. I'm sorry, but if Oliver and Wendell have problems with us, I want to fix it. C'mon, Darryl, please indulge me on this."

"How does the app work?"

"When they're within fifty feet of the open app, it picks up their brainwaves, translates them into English, and sends a transcript to my email. If we use this app, we'll find out what the cats really think about us."

"It sounds like a lot of work."

"Not really. I'll just put a phone on the dresser in the guest bedroom where the cats like to hang out. Then later in the day, I'll check my email for the transcripts of messages they send to each other. You don't have to do anything."

"Cat Chat, huh? It just sounds hokey."

"Please, Darryl, humor me. Can I get you on board with this?"

"What does it cost?"

"There's a one-year subscription for $399, but if we can cancel within thirty days, it's completely free."

"All right. Do it. But I think you're just wasting your time."

\*\*\*\*\*

After dinner, Julie logged onto the Cat Chat website. She filled out some basic information about the cats, including their names and ages. After providing her credit-card info, Julie downloaded the app to her phone.

Now she would find out what the cats truly thought of her and Darryl. And maybe if they planned to bury her alive in cat litter.

## Chapter 5

When Julie got home from work the next day, she immediately checked her email, opened the attachment from Cat Chat, and printed out the transcript. She carried it to the family room where Darryl was reclined on the couch, snacking on chips, and watching *Access Hollywood.*

"Listen, Darryl, we received the first cat conversation back from Cat Chat. It's surprising and very interesting."

Darryl pressed the mute button for the TV. "You're kidding? What did those stupid cats talk about? I mean, what did they discuss 'telepathically'?"

"It looks like the program has figured out which thoughts belong to each cat because they've designated each piece of dialogue to either 'O' for Oliver or 'W' for Wendell. I'll read it. It starts with a message from Elon Musk."

### Message From Elon Musk, CEO of Cat Chat

Welcome fellow cat owner! I developed this feline brainwave-analysis program during my spare time last year while I was vacationing on one of my private islands. I can't remember which island because I was pretty high at the time. I do remember palm trees, sea turtles, and a mermaid with long blonde hair though. Just kidding; there were no sea turtles. But,

I digress. This project started when I became curious about whether my two cats, Morpheus and Capricorn-X, would like to travel with me on my first SpaceX flight to Mars, now scheduled for June 28, 2041. But in creating the program, I soon realized this new software could help humanity by allowing all cat owners to understand their cats' thoughts, interests, and motivations. If I make a lot of money in the process, of course I'll give it all to a worthy charity. LOL. After developing this program, it dawned on me that both my cats will be dead by the time my spaceship goes to Mars, but maybe Cat Chat could still benefit humanity. Be prepared to find out a lot about your fur babies, maybe more than you ever wanted to know. LOL. Elon

### January 10   2:37 p.m.

**Oliver:** "*Hola, amigo.* How are you?"

**Wendell:** "In a bit of a funk, *amigo.*"

**O:** "What's wrong?"

**W:** "While staring out the window, I had an epiphany."

**O:** "What was it?"

**W:** "I have a strong feeling there's something more to life than what's inside this house."

**O:** "I don't understand."

**W:** "Well, for a couple of months we've lived a quiet, contented life here. We get our three squares a day, we have numerous comfy places to sleep, and there are countless toys."

**O:** "So what's the problem?"

**W:** "I just have this deep feeling I'm missing out on something. This thought comes to me while I stare out the window. There's another world out there, yet I know very little about it. Do you ever feel this way, *amigo?*"

**O:** "Sometimes."

**W:** "I also wonder about my purpose. Why am I here? What does it all mean? What should I be doing? And other nagging questions."

**O:** "Ugh. I was having such a good day until now."

**W:** "Sorry to bring you down, *amigo*. But these questions haunt me. Don't you ever ponder the great questions of the universe?"

**O:** "Sure. I often wonder, 'Why is there *something* instead of *nothing*?'"

**W:** "That's an excellent question."

**O:** "And why is the sky blue?"

**W:** "I wonder that too, *amigo*."

**O:** "Which came first, the chicken or the egg?"

**W:** "Wow. You are full of profound questions."

**O:** "Then there's the ultimate stumper: How do you fold a fitted sheet?"

**W:** "Ah, good one. Just be thankful you'll never need to."


Julie said, "What do think, Darryl? Isn't that interesting?"

"I don't know. Why would you even attempt to fold a fitted sheet? I mean just scrunch it up into a tight ball and stuff it into the linen closet. And how do you know Elon didn't just make this up?"

"No, what I thought was interesting was our cats pondering the meaning of life. And sure, Musk is brilliant, but no one could make this kind of stuff up."

Darryl chugged some beer. "Eh, sounds boring to me. And what's with calling each other '*amigo*'? Are they Mexican cats?"

"Maybe their previous owners spoke Spanish."

"And what's a 'piffeny'? Is that Spanish too?"

"Epiphany means a revelation of some kind."

"Huh. Well I have revelation for you: These cats are bored and need to get a life."

Julie rolled her eyes. "Okay then Mr. Smarty-pants, what do *you* propose?"

"I don't know. Let's give them mini backpacks and send them out to explore the world. Maybe they can go south of the border and practice their Spanish. What do *you* propose?"

"There's obviously a lot of discontentment, at least with Wendell. I think we keep using Cat Chat to get more insight into their thoughts and feelings."

"Okay, Dr. Freud. Whatever you say."

## Chapter 6

Julie printed out the two transcripts from the second day of Cat Chat and carried them downstairs. She found Darryl on the couch in the family room. "Will you stop watching *The Simpsons* and listen to what the cats said today?"

"I wasn't actually watching; the cats like the show."

Julie looked at Wendell and Oliver. They were both planted a few feet in front of the TV with their heads tilted upward and their eyes glued to the screen. "You're kidding? Then why are they hissing?"

"I know it's weird. They're mesmerized by the show, but they don't seem to like Homer and Bart."

"So you turn it on for them every day?"

"Yep. It keeps them out of my hair, what's left of it. So tell me what our feline philosophers said today. Have they discussed us yet?"

"Yes, and it's not good."

"Uh oh. What'd they say?"

"Let's leave the room, so the cats don't hear us." Darryl followed Julie into the kitchen where she softly read the first transcript.

O: "*Amigo*, have you ever sat on the newspaper while Blondie was reading it?"

W: "Sure. If I'm bored or feeling a bit mischievous, I'll deliberately sit on the article Blondie's reading. And surprisingly, she doesn't make me move. She just tries to read around me. I figure she must think I'm trying to get attention. She has no idea I'm just messing with her. It's hilarious."

O: "I know. It's so bizarre that she lets me block her reading. More often than not, she'll even pet me while I'm sitting there."

W: "Just a warning, I tried the same stunt once with Dagwood, and he swatted me with an oven mitt."

O: "Yeah, I tried it with Dagwood too and got a similar unhinged response."

W: "It's funny, we think of humans as all being alike. But they really do have different personalities."


Darryl said, "They call us, 'Blondie and Dagwood'?"

"Patricia Van Winkle said they had given us insulting nicknames. I suppose it could be a lot worse."

"Why do you let the cats sit on your newspaper?"

"It's kind of cute when they do it. I thought they just wanted to be near me and didn't think it was a prank."

"It seems like Oliver and Wendell don't respect us much."

"That was nothing. Wait 'til you hear what they said about us in this next conversation."


January 11 2:07 p.m.

O: "If Blondie and Dagwood got divorced who would you go with?"

W: "I don't think we'd really have a choice. It's whichever one of those yokels wants us."

O: "But if you could choose, who would you pick?"

W: "Not sure. They both have pros and cons."

O: "Yeah, like Dagwood ignores us most of the time, so that's one in his favor."

W: "True. But he also yells at us when we claw the furniture."

19

O: "Blondie feeds us without fail, one in her favor."

W: "But it's always the expired bland crap she gets from the discount bin."

O: "Dagwood seems oblivious when we chew plant leaves in front of him."

W: "But he threw a shoe at me the other day when I was pooping in the potted plant."

O: "Blondie speaks affectionately to us."

W: "But she also picks us up and kisses us, a huge negative in her column."

O: "Dagwood cuts the cheese in front of us and never apologizes or cracks a window."

W: "Speaking of foul odors, Blondie wears that god-awful perfume."

O: "Dagwood lets us drink his beer."

W: "But it's always some crappy brand, never the good stuff."

O: "It's like choosing between a rock and a hard place. I'd rather go back to the shelter."

W: "Me too. Any other owner would be an improvement."

O: "Or, hear me out: We go live with Chiquita Bonita."

W: "Now you're talking."

Julie said, "Ouch, that's painful to read. They'd prefer new owners. I guess there's no longer any doubt. Our cats hate us."

"Those ingrates. After everything we do for them, they want to live somewhere else."

"Maybe if we keep using Cat Chat we can figure out how to win them over."

Darryl laughed. "Good luck with that."

"What do you think they meant about going to 'live with 'Chiquita Bonita.'?"

"I'm guessing the app just mistranslated. They probably said something else, like 'let's go—eat a chocolate burrito.'"

Julie rolled her eyes. "Yeah, that makes so much more sense."

## Chapter 7

The next afternoon, Darryl called his former coworker from his old construction job, Rowdy Phillips. "Hey, dude. How's the eight-to-five grind?"

"You're a funny man, Darryl Belcher. Right now I'm standing ankle-deep in sewage, freezing my acorns off, and about to pass out from the fumes. Does that answer your question?"

"Ahh, the good ole days of installing sewer pipes. I miss it."

"I'll bet you do. You're just lucky you won the lottery and can retire."

"You got it all wrong, Rowdy. I'm not retired; I'm way too young to retire."

"Then what are you doing?"

"I told you, dude. I'm a professional gambler now."

"For real? I thought you were joking."

After swallowing a mouth full of potato chips and a sip of beer, Darryl said, "Nope. This is serious business. I play online poker every day, and I hit Lucky Star Casino at least twice a week."

"Do you think you can actually make a career out of just playing poker?"

"I'm not just playing poker. I'm also dabbling in blackjack, and I just downloaded the apps for Draft Kings and Fan Duel. Sports betting is right up my alley. I think it'll be extremely lucrative."

"Wow. You went whole hog. Have you made any money yet?"

"Not yet. I'm still learning the ropes on poker and blackjack and just started placing sports bets. Truthfully, I ran into a little bad luck, but things will turn around. There's a learning curve, but I'm sure I'll get there."

"Where do you bet the most?"

"So far I've spread it around evenly. Investment experts call it 'diversification.'"

Rowdy climbed out of the sewer to get better reception. "What does Julie think about your new career?"

"She doesn't like it, but she doesn't say much. What can she say? It's my money."

"I wish my wife were that understanding. If I gambled every day, she'd cut off my johnson."

"Julie doesn't exactly approve, but she'll come around. Especially when I start winning big."

"Seriously though, how long are you going to give this so-called gambling career? You know the odds are against you, right?"

Darryl brushed potato-chip crumbs off his shirt. "I disagree. I think the odds are excellent. I'll give it as long as it takes. Although I'm in a bit of a hole, I'm having a blast. It's a lot more fun than construction."

"Yeah, I'm sure it is. I envy you. I'll go to the casino with you sometime. I wouldn't mind playing some blackjack."

"You're on, dude. I'll let you know next time I go."

"Can you share any gambling advice with me?"

Darryl reflected for a moment. "Just one tip. Don't sit down at a gaming table if you're drunk. You'll make dumb bets."

"Makes sense."

"I'm speaking from lots of experience."

*Season's Greetings*

## Chapter 8

After arriving home from work, Julie printed out the day's Cat Chat conversations. She was surprised to see three separate transcripts. She carried the papers downstairs to the family room, shutting the door behind her. "Three more cat conversations. You want to hear them?"

Darryl hit the mute button to silence *Friends*. "I wasn't crazy about their criticisms yesterday. I hope they're easier on me today."

"That's debatable. I'll let you decide. Here's the first one, which doesn't even mention you."

**January 12  9:12 a.m.**

**O:** "Have you gotten over the reindeer antlers?"

**W:** "Ugh. I can't believe they put those stupid things on us for a photo. It's further proof Blondie is trying to emasculate us."

23

O: "Well, I wouldn't dwell on it. After all, Christmas is just once a year. Then it's over."

W: "Hardly. That lame photo will live forever on the internet. I'll always be the laughing stock of the cat community."

O: "And me along with you."

W: "Is there a worse holiday than Christmas?"

O: "Halloween kind of sucks."

W: "Yeah, that devil costume really itches."

Darryl laughed. "That's so funny. Who knew our cats hated getting dressed up?"

"For one, I knew. I could tell they hated those costumes. They always squirmed when I put them on. Maybe we shouldn't dress them up anymore."

"No way. We've got to keep doing it. Those pictures are hilarious and people love them."

"True, but now we know how the cats feel. Here's the next conversation. You're not going to like it."

**January 12  1:23 p.m.**

W: "I saw you playing with Dagwood earlier."

O: "Really? I'm embarrassed you saw me. It was a weak moment on my part."

W: "What was going on?"

O: "Dagwood was obviously bored and tried to engage me in some play. No big deal."

W: "Were you having fun?"

O: "God no. I was just humoring the guy. He insisted on playing, and I gave in."

W: "But he's such a loser."

O: "I know, which is why I couldn't help feeling sorry for him."

W: "Did you get a whiff of his feet today?"

O: "Yes, quite atrocious. I wish he would change his socks more than once a week."

W: "How long did you play with him?"

O: "Not long. After a few minutes I slithered under the couch so he couldn't bother me."

Darryl said, "They have a lot of nerve calling *me* a loser. They just sleep all day...in my house."

"Our house."

"Yeah, whatever. Read the last one."

"This last conversation is very short."

**January 12  4:02 p.m.**

**W:** "Wouldn't it be great if we didn't have to see them anymore?"

**O:** "You mean eliminate them somehow?"

**W:** "Yes, eliminate them."

**O:** "Just not sure how we would do it."

**W:** "There might be a way. Let's sleep on it."

Julie said, "That's a weird conversation. What could they want to eliminate?"

"Maybe their gambling debts?"

"No, that's something *you'd* want. I'll be very interested to see what they say tomorrow."

Darryl groaned. "Not me. I'm not sure I want to hear anymore conversations. These cats are unappreciative freeloaders, and I resent being called a loser."

"My parents call you a loser all the time."

"Yeah, but I'm used to hearing it from them."

## Chapter 9

After dinner the next night, Julie downloaded the day's new conversations and carried the transcripts into the bedroom where Darryl was stretched out on the bed watching a hockey game. "Did you have a rough day at work, honey? Oh, excuse me. I mean a rough day doing nothing."

"Not 'nothing.' I did a load of laundry. Why are you bugging me?"

Julie sat at the end of the bed. "We have two more cat conversations today. Well, actually three. The third one is very short and cryptic."

Darryl hit the mute button and said, "Okay, let's hear 'em."

```
January 13  9:31 a.m.
W: "See that water stain on the ceiling?"
O: "Yeah, what about it?"
W: "Does it remind you of anything?"
```

```
O: "Nopc."

W: "Look at it closely."

O: "Oh my god. Yes! It looks just like Napoleon."

W: "No, look at it from over here. Now who do you see?"

O: "Um, Abraham Lincoln?"

W: "No, that's not it either. Try tilting your head to the
right. Now who does it look like?"

O: "Oh, I see it now. It's Jesus."

W: "No. Try tilting your head even further."

O: "Nope, I still see Jesus. He even has a halo."

W: "Wrong again."

O: "All right, smartass, tell me. Who am I supposed to
see?"

W: "It's Grampa Simpson. I can't believe you don't see
it."

O: "No, I think you're wrong. It's Jesus no matter how I
look at it."

W: "You are hopeless. Just forget it."
```

Julie dropped the transcripts to her side, gazed at Darryl, and said, "This is unbelievable."

"I know. I can't believe you still haven't painted that water stain. It's embarrassing."

Julie grabbed Darryl's arm. "No, not the water stain. How about the fact that our cats somehow know Napoleon, Lincoln, and Jesus?"

"So we got cats who are history buffs. There are worse things."

"And how do they know Grampa Simpson?"

"I told you, they seem to like *The Simpsons*. So I have it on almost every day."

Julie gave Darryl a cold stare. "Okay, here's the next conversation."

```
January 13  11:57 a.m.

O: "I haven't seen any empty boxes around here lately."

W: "I know. Last box I remember was the one that held the
microwave."

O: "Yeah, about three weeks ago. That was fun."

W: "It would be nice if Dagwood and Blondie would order
more stuff on Amazon, so we'd have more boxes to jump in."
```

**O:** "I don't get it. They're Prime members, so you'd think boxes would be delivered to the house every day.

**W:** "Dagwood is a real cheapskate. Maybe he's gotten on Blondie's case for ordering too much crap."

**O:** "But Dagwood orders his share of crap. Remember the huge clown clock he bought last year?"

**W:** "Hideous. It was hanging on the wall for like five seconds before Blondie took it off and made Dagwood return it."

**O:** "And how 'bout his orange beanbag chair?"

**W:** What an eyesore. Fortunately it hasn't left the basement."

**O:** "Oh, remember the framed poster Dagwood got?"

**W:** "Dogs playing poker? Quite tacky."

**O:** "I was snooping in the hall closet a few weeks ago and found that picture."

**W:** "Notice anything odd about it?"

**O:** "Yeah, it smelled funky."

**W:** "I peed on it."


Darryl said, "Why didn't you let me hang that poster? It would look great over the fireplace."

"Sadly, my cats have better taste in decorating than my husband."

"You just don't appreciate great art. When I win my first poker tournament, will you let me hang it?"

"Eww. You still want to hang it, knowing it's been peed on? All right, here's the next transcript."


### January 13   3:38 p.m.

**W:** "So what do you think, *amigo*?"

**O:** "I think you're right. We need to get rid of them."

**W:** "Good. Now we just need to come up with a plan."

**O:** "Once the deed is done, do we stay here or get the hell out of Dodge?"

**W:** "I think we'll need to get as far away from this dump as humanly possible."

**O:** "Why'd you say 'humanly possible' instead of 'catly possible'?"

**W:** "Nobody says 'catly possible.' It sounds awkward."

**O:** "Okay. So once we're out of here, will we stay together or split up?"

**W:** "You're putting me on the spot, *amigo*. For now, let's just worry about coming up with a good plan to put our troubles behind us."


Julie said, "What are they talking about? Why would they call our house a dump? It's not a palace, but it's certainly not a dump."

"Nor do we live in Dodge. Maybe they're communicating in some secret cat code."

"They don't own anything, so what would they get rid of?"

"Oh, I know. Maybe the reindeer antlers?"

"You think?"

"It's the only thing that makes sense."

Julie felt a shiver go down her spine. "Or maybe, they want to get rid of us."

"Nah, that can't be true." Darryl felt their dog, Max, nuzzle against his leg and reached down to pet his head. "Hey Max, you know the cats well. What do you think? Do they want to get rid of us? Bark once for yes or twice for no. What do you think, boy? Max looked up at Darryl, farted, and walked away.

## Chapter 10

Later that night, Julie sat at the kitchen counter with a sprouts sandwich and Diet Coke. After two bites she called Linda.

"Hey, Sis. I learned something amazing in the last couple of days. It's going to sound totally nuts, but I had to tell someone."

"What?"

"Our cats are super smart, like geniuses."

"I'm sorry. I think I misheard you. Did you say your cats are 'geniuses'?"

Julie sipped her Coke. "I did. What would you say if I told you our cats know about Napoleon, Lincoln, and Jesus?"

"I'd say you're eating too many pot gummies."

"Not true. I've only had two in the last several days. Listen, I've been recording the cats using a new app that translates their brainwaves into English."

"Ha. You're joking, right?"

"No, this is for real. There's an app that can read cats' thoughts called Cat Chat."

"Sounds unbelievable. Are you sure it's legit?"

"Yes. Elon Musk came up with the app in his spare time so he could learn whether his cats would like to go to Mars with him. So you know it works."

"Elon Musk has spare time?"

"Apparently so."

"How do you know that your cats know all those famous people?"

As Julie bit her sandwich, a glob of mayo fell into her lap. *Crap.* "You know that water stain on the ceiling in the guest bedroom? The one that's been there awhile?"

"The one that looks like Grampa Simpson?"

"Wendell thinks so too. But Oliver thinks it looks like Napoleon, Lincoln, and Jesus."

"He saw all of those people in one water stain? Are you sure Oliver isn't eating gummies along with you?"

"No, he thinks it looks like three different people from different angles."

"Are you pulling my leg? I'm still waiting for the punch line."

"There is no punch line. These cats are extremely intelligent. Wendell was even pondering the meaning of life a couple of days ago. It was quite profound. I'm telling you our cats are super smart, smarter than you'd ever think."

"I guess that makes up for your husband."

"That was mean, but I can't argue. They'd probably clobber Darryl in an IQ test."

"So what are you going to do, get your cats on *Jeopardy*?"

Julie reflected for a moment. "I don't know what to do. I just had to tell somebody."

"Thanks for picking me, but I'm not quite sure what to make of it."

"Oh, I almost forgot, the cats thought the dogs-playing-poker poster was tacky."

Linda laughed. "They obviously have better taste than the guy who bought it."

"That's what I told Darryl."

"Listen, Sis, I'd like to believe you, but it does sounds wacky. You might want to keep the whole 'cats being geniuses' to yourself."

"You're probably right. Don't say anything to anyone either."

"I promise I won't. The last thing I want is for people to think I'm related to a mental case." *Having Darryl in our family is bad enough.*

## Chapter 11

Julie strolled into the family room, transcripts in hand. "Okay, here are today's conversations."

"I'm tired of hearing these indignant cats insult me."

"You might enjoy this first conversation. There's nothing about you, but they make fun of me."

"Sold. Let's hear it."

Julie read the first transcript.

**January 14   8:41 a.m.**

O: "Lately I've been aloof toward Blondie. I mean more than usual."

W: "Why?"

O: "Sometimes she just bores me. Don't get me wrong, Blondie's an okay lady. But I'm a cat, I need my space."

W: "Copy that."

O: "And it gets worse. She'll speak to me like I'm an infant."

**W:** "Exactly. Her voice goes a few octaves higher when she talks to me. It's like baby talk."

**O:** "She'll say, 'Oliver, you're such a fuzzy wuzzy cutie pootie pie.' I mean what the hell? I'm a four-year-old mature adult cat, not some dumb little kitten."

**W:** "Yep, she does that with me too. It's so friggin' annoying."

**O:** "Anyway, *amigo*, I've tried to deal with this excessive attention by acting indifferent. You know, like I just don't care about Blondie. But, for some reason, it only makes her more affectionate."

**W:** "Yeah, humans always want what they can't have."

**O:** "What a pathetic species."

Julie finished reading, lowered the transcript to her side, and said, "I'm in shock. Can you believe their language? It's so mean and coarse. Do cats really say the F-word?"

"Friggin'? Of course not. They don't actually *say* it. They *think* it."

Julie looked at Darryl. "But doesn't that surprise you?"

"Eh, not really. They always seem a bit irritated to me. I get the 'F-you' look from Wendell quite a bit."

"I do too. That's what I told Linda a few weeks ago."

"He even gave me that look five minutes ago when I squirted him with the water bottle so he'd get off the kitchen counter."

"After all the love I've given them, I just can't believe our cats don't like me." Julie sighed and read the second transcript.

**January 14  12:26 p.m.**

**W:** "B and S have to go."

**O:** "Agreed. They are so obnoxious."

**W:** "One is incredibly dumb, and the other is an annoying smartass."

**O:** "Their voices are like fingernails on a blackboard."

**W:** "But how do we get rid of them?"

**O:** "We need to figure out a plan."

Julie said, "That's where it ends. Do you need any more evidence that the cats hate us?"

"I don't think they're talking about us. B and S aren't our initials. Besides, neither of us are obnoxious. Or at least I'm not."

"You want a second opinion? Here's the next conversation. Maybe you can shed some light on this one."

**January 14   3:10 p.m.**

O: "Chiquita Bonita was here today."

W: "Dagwood's good friend? Yeah, I saw her."

O: "She's nice, but talks funny."

W: "Yeah, kind of a high-pitched voice."

O: "She seems to like Dagwood."

W: "Yes, they're very chummy."

O: "I like the way she speaks *Español*."

W: "*Si, la muchacha habla Español muy bien.*

O: "On the other hand, Dagwood *es un doofus grande.*

W: "But for some reason Chiquita Bonita likes him."

O: "Another mystery of the universe."

Darryl said, "That does it. The cats are leaving tomorrow."

"The cats aren't going anywhere. And by the way, who the heck is Chiquita Bonita?"

Darryl looked at his phone and pretended to be distracted. "How should I know?"

"They said, 'Chiquita Bonita is Dagwood's good friend, and they're 'very chummy.'"

"These cats are delusional. They probably saw something on TV, maybe an interview with Sophia Vergara."

"Huh. It's all just very weird. I still wonder what they meant about getting out of Dodge."

"I can easily make their wish come true. Just give me the word, and they'll soon be living in a forest twenty miles from here."

"Before we relocate them, let's see if we can find out more about their grievances. Maybe we can turn them around so they like me."

"What about *me*?"

"That might take longer."

## Chapter 12

Julie walked into the family room and looked around. "Where are the cats?"

While texting, Darryl said, "I don't know. Somewhere, not here."

Julie shut the door. "There are three more cat conversations, but first a message from Mr. Musk."

"I'm listening."

"Are you?"

"Not really. But go ahead and read them anyway."

# Message From Elon Musk, CEO of Cat Chat

Please excuse my appearance. I was up all night trying to figure out how to save Twitter. I thought renaming it something cool like "X" would turn things around. Hmm. Maybe I should have picked a different letter. LOL. Fortunately, I may have found the solution. I've just laid off all the employees except for three high school kids. Now I'll probably be accused of nepotism just because all three kids are mine. Anyway, I hope you're having more fun with Cat Chat than I'm having with Twitter...I mean X. For me, Cat Chat has truly opened up a window into my cats' lives. For example, I recently learned that my Siamese, Capricorn-X, is a big fan of Greek philosophy, especially the writings of Aristotle. Whereas my Persian, Morpheus, has been studying physics and theories of multidimensional universes. Yes, I know what you're thinking. Were they naturally interested in those subjects, or did I encourage those studies like an overbearing parent? I plead guilty. LOL. Anyway I wanted to remind you that there are only a few weeks left on your free membership before your paid membership kicks in. Okay, gotta run. I have some fires to put out at SpaceX. Literally. The jet-propulsion lab is on fire. Later. Elon

## January 15   10:09 a.m.

**W:** "What was that commotion in the kitchen this morning?"

**O:** "Oh, you heard that? I found a grape on the floor and started batting it around. It was exhilarating. That grape was rolling all over the place."

**W:** "I almost caught a mouse a couple of weeks ago."

**O:** "Hey. Hey. Hey. I wasn't done with my grape story. It's not polite to interrupt. I don't interrupt your stories."

**W:** "Oh, excuse me. I thought you were done. Please continue."

**O:** "Well anyway, I batted the grape under the cabinet where it was totally out of reach. Looking under the cabinet, I could see the grape, but as hard as I tried, I couldn't reach it. Just couldn't reach it. I checked a couple of minutes ago, and the grape is still there. Wild, huh?"

**W:** "Is that the whole story? Are you done?"

**O:** "Yeah, I'm done."

**W:** "Well, that's quite a story. One epic tale. I'm terribly sorry I interrupted."

**O:** "Let's not be sarcastic."

**W:** "When does the movie come out?"

**O:** "Why are you being such a dick?"

**W:** "I'm just saying, it's not that great a story."

**O:** "It's better than your I-almost-caught-a-mouse story."

**W:** "What do you mean? I like my mouse story."

**O:** "You know what would make an even better story? If you actually caught the damn mouse. *Almost* catching a mouse is not a good story."

**W:** "I disagree."

**O:** "Besides you already told me the I-almost-caught-a-mouse story a couple of times already."

**W:** "If I told it to you before, why didn't you say something when I told it again?"

**O:** "I was just being polite. That's what nice cats do."

**W:** "Oh, screw you. Next time you have a boring story about chasing a grape, just keep it to yourself."


Darryl said, "I kind of enjoy hearing them insult each other. It softens the sting of their jabs at me."

"Did you know there was a mouse in the house?"

"Elmo? Yeah, he's been coming and going for several weeks."

Julie scowled. "You *named* him? Did you ever try to catch him?"

"Nah. I figure that's the cats' job. I don't want to interfere with their duties. They hate me enough."

"Ugh. Here's the second one."

**January 15   1:35 p.m.**

**O:** "I saw you sitting on Blondie's lap yesterday."

**W:** "Yeah, I'll hop on her lap every now and then."

**O:** "Do you enjoy it?"

**W:** "It's all right. I can tell she likes me sitting there, so I'll indulge her. Plus I often get a head massage, which relieves some stress."

**O:** "You were purring."

**W:** "No way, José. You'll never catch this bad boy purring."

**O:** "Hmm...I thought I heard you."

**W:** "You were mistaken."

**O:** "If you say so. Just curious, have you ever sat on Dagwood's lap?"

**W:** "Ugh. Yes, I sat on his lap once a couple of months ago."

**O:** "How was it?"

**W:** "Traumatic. He sneezed on me, a tsunami sneeze. Didn't even bother to warn me or cover his mouth. After that, I vowed never to go near his lap."

**O:** "That's so disgusting. Was it as traumatic as when he puked on you?"

**W:** "My Dagwood traumas are all bad, but I do have the most nightmares about the sneeze."


Darryl said, "I don't remember either cat ever sitting on my lap. I think Wendell is making up the sneeze part."

"I believe him. I remember one time we were talking in bed and you sneezed directly at me. You sprayed me so thoroughly that I had to take a shower."

"That must have been my hay fever."

"Well, you might want to remember to cover your mouth. Even the cats are repulsed."

"You and the cats are all nutty germophobes. What's the next conversation?"

"It's the last one, and it's weird. Well, even weirder."


**January 15   4:26 p.m.**

**W:** "How's your grape doing? Is it still cowering under the cabinet?"

**O:** "Funny. Have you *almost* caught any mice lately?"

**W:** "All right. Enough. Let's call a truce."

**O:** "Fine with me."

**W:** "Care to brainstorm a bit?"

**O:** "About what?"

**W:** "Getting rid of you know who."

**O:** "You mean 'off' them?"

**W:** "Did you just say 'off them'? Who are you, Tony Soprano?"

**O:** "'Off them' sounds sort of cool. Like something a gangster would say."

**W:** "You need to stop watching so many Martin Scorsese movies. I'm just waiting to hear you say 'whack them.'"

**O:** "Ooh, I like that. Let's whack them. Bada-bing."


"Darryl, why do you let the cats watch so many mobster movies? Look what it's done to them."

"How is this *my* fault? A week ago I didn't even think cats had brains, let alone could comprehend movie plots."

Her voice cracking, Julie said, "Well obviously they can, and all these movies have made murder seem appealing."

"Yeah, but they can't possibly mean it? Maybe they're just pretending to be tough guys."

"I hope you're right. It's troubling to think the cats are planning a murder, and even more troubling to think we could be their targets."

## Chapter 13

The next afternoon Julie said, "Here's the first conversation from earlier today."

"I hope there's nothing more about 'offing' somebody."

"No, but these conversations aren't going to make us feel any better."

Darryl sighed. "They never do. Let's get it over with."

**January 16  12:48 p.m.**

**W:** "I noticed you're grooming that one area a lot."

**O:** "What?"

**W:** "It just seems like you've been grooming your chest excessively today. Maybe a bit compulsively, if you ask me."

**O:** "I don't know what you're implying. I don't have OCD or anything like that."

**W:** "Just my observation, that's all."

**O:** "Well, if you must know, I'm nursing a sore spot."

**W:** "Oh, how'd that happen?"

**O:** "Remember when we were tussling earlier today? You jumped on me pretty hard."

**W:** "We were just fooling around, friendly horseplay."

**O:** "I know, but sometimes you go a bit overboard. You really nailed my sternum. It hurts like a son of a bitch."

**W:** "I'm so sorry. I didn't realize you were such a delicate flower."

**O:** "C'mon. I could nail you just as hard, but I'm a little more considerate."

**W:** "Right. You're always so considerate. You didn't even bury your poop in the litter box this morning."

**O:** "Give me a break. I was in a hurry."

Julie said, "That's the end of the conversation. They seem to argue about everything."

"Gee, I wonder who they learned that habit from."

"Are you blaming me for our cats being quarrelsome?"

"Just saying, I know they didn't get it from me. You're the one who picks a fight over every little thing. What you'd scold me for at dinner last night: that I was talking while chewing?"

"You were spitting chunks of chicken onto the table."

"Just a couple of times."

"I counted seven. Anyway, here's the last transcript. It's very short. I'm not even going to read it."

"Give it to me. I'll read it." Darryl reached over, grabbed the transcript from Julie's hand, and read it out loud.

**January 16  2:27 p.m.**

**O:** "Who was that tall tattooed guy last night?"

**W:** "Don't know. Blondie was very friendly with him though."

**O:** "He talks funny."

**W:** "I think he's Eastern European, maybe Russian."

**O:** "Why was he here?"

**W:** "You got me. I don't like the dude though. He stared at me and said, 'In my country we eat cats for breakfast' and then laughed menacingly."

**O:** "That is spooky. Do you think he was telling the truth?"

41

**W:** "I doubt it, but just to be safe, I plan to hide if he ever comes over at breakfast time."

**O:** "I'm right behind you, *amigo*."


Darryl said, "What the heck are they talking about?"

"You got me. I have no idea. I don't know any Russians. It's probably a sinister character they saw on TV."

"Are you telling the truth? You always avert your eyes when you lie."

Julie locked eyes with Darryl and said, "I don't know any Russians. I'm not having an affair with a Russian. Okay, satisfied?"

"Hmm...what about a Belarusian?"

## Chapter 14

After Darryl left for the casino that evening, Julie poured a glass of wine and called Linda.

"Hey, Julie. How's it going?"

"Eh. Don't ask."

"What's wrong?"

"Oh, Linda, I'm so frustrated. I've just about had it with Darryl."

"What's he done this time?"

Julie sighed. "It's this so-called new career of his. He thinks he can make a living by playing poker and blackjack. It's just insane."

"How often does he go to the casino?"

"At least three or four times a week. In fact, he's there now. Plus, when he's home, he's playing online poker most of the time. And in the last two weeks, he's been betting on sports. I'm just worried he's going to bankrupt us."

"Well, it's his money he's spending, right?"

Julie sipped her wine. "Sort of. But isn't it also my money too? I mean we're married, so I should have some say in the spending."

"How much has he lost?"

"I've asked him several times, but he won't tell me. He always says he 'almost won big,' or he's 'overdue for a big jackpot.' I know he's squandered thousands of dollars. I just don't know exactly how much."

"Wow. Do you think he would've become a professional gambler if he hadn't won the lottery?"

"No way. In gambling, it takes money to make money. And he had very little in the bank until he won the million."

"Have you told him how you feel and that maybe he should go back to working construction?"

Julie sighed. "Yeah, we've had those arguments. Thing is, winning the lottery has gone completely to his head. He now thinks he was born to be a professional gambler. He hears about how some people win millions of dollars a year playing poker, and he thinks he can do the same thing."

"But the lottery was just dumb luck, wasn't it? There's no skill involved."

"Of course. But when I point that out, he doesn't listen. To him, winning the lottery by picking the uniform numbers of his favorite football players is somehow proof that he's got a gift for gambling. He's convinced it's his calling."

"How long are you going to let him play out this fantasy?"

"I don't really have a choice. I wish I could force him to quit, but he's not a child, although he acts like one."

Linda finally asked the question she often wanted to ask: "Truthfully, would you have married Darryl if he hadn't won the lottery?"

"Yes. I know you don't think much of Darryl, but he was much nicer, even sweet, before he won the lottery. Unfortunately, winning the big prize has made him lazy and cocky."

"On the plus side, I'll bet he's not as cheap as he was before he won."

"You would lose that bet. He's much worse. He complains about every nickel we spend. Yet it's fine for him to flush thousands down the toilet in his delusional quest to be the world's best poker player."

"I'm sorry he's caused you so much distress."

Julie took a deep breath. "I try to think positive. Marriage is for better or worse. Maybe I'm just getting the worse over with early."

"Sure, Julie, that's probably it." *I give them six months at best.*

## Chapter 15

Julie held up the day's Cat Chat conversations and said, "These are interesting. Fortunately, there's not much in here about you or me. But they do ridicule Max and each other."

Darryl said, "So no mention of their contempt for a Russian who eats cats?"

"Nope. Just making fun of Max."

"That sounds funny. I'd like to hear that."

Julie read the first transcript.

**January 18  9:55 a.m.**

**W:** "I was sleeping on the couple's bed this morning when I was rudely awakened."

**O:** "What happened?"

**W:** "Max was licking me."

**O:** "What'd you do?"

**W:** "At first I tried to ignore him, but I couldn't take it. His breath was disgusting."

**O:** "Yeah, it's god-awful. So you walked away?"

W: "Hell no. I hissed and swiped at him with my claws out. He got the message. A second later, he was out the door with his tail between his legs."

O: "Poor guy. He's probably just trying to be friendly."

W: "True, but he was out of line with the licking. I had to put him in his place."

O: "You need to cut him some slack, *amigo*. He's just a dumb animal and forgets the chain of command."


Darryl said, "They seem a bit full of themselves. They probably think we're beneath them in the chain of command."

"Possibly, but I'll tell you this much, they're frustrated with the laser light, which might help keep them humble. Listen to this next conversation."


**January 18  11:01 a.m.**

O: "Do think the red dot will show up tonight?"

W: "Maybe. We haven't seen it for several nights, so it's overdue."

O: "I sure hope it shows up. I was on the verge of catching it last week. Came so close."

W: "Me too. I pounced on it and thought I had it, but it was gone."

O: "Actually I've come very close many times, but just when I catch up with it, it somehow eludes me. Time and time again, I've come up empty. It's maddening."

W: "Yeah, it's wild how it always escapes."

O: "The day after the red dot appears, I'm often haunted by it. It's all I can think about."

W: "Me too. That red dot is my *white whale*."

O: "Maybe we should try harpooning it."

W: "You're hilarious."

O: "Seriously, we could try trapping it."

W: "How, with food? What do you think it eats?"

O: "It's very small. A bread crumb would probably feed it for a month."

W: "I think it's too clever to be trapped with food. I just wish I knew its motivation for showing up."

O: "Maybe there's some info on the internet."

**W:** "Good idea. Remind me to Google, 'How do you catch a red dot?'"

Julie said, "How do they even know about the white whale? That is so bizarre."

"Easy explanation. I was watching the movie *Flipper* a couple of months ago. I'm sure they picked it up from that."

"Flipper's a dolphin."

"Dolphin, whale...whatever. Cats are too stupid to know the difference. They're both just big fish to them."

"Not so sure. I'll bet our cats are so smart they could tell us who wrote *Moby Dick* and the year it was written."

"If they're so smart, why are they still fooled by the red dot?"

"Good point."

## Chapter 16

Julie walked into the bedroom and shut the door. "I printed out today's cat conversations."

Darryl rolled over on the bed. "Ugh, I was having a great day until you walked in."

"What made it a great day?"

"I didn't lose very much today. In fact, I almost came out ahead in blackjack. If I had only quit a half an hour earlier..."

Julie sat on the bed. "I'm sorry to interrupt your 'great' day. I just want you to hear these two new conversations. Wendell snooped in the kitchen and discovered the catnip. Listen."

**January 19  1:36 p.m.**

W: "Good news, *amigo*."

O: "What?"

W: "I found out where they're hiding the dope."

O: "No kidding? Did you partake?"

W: "Of course. I sniffed for a few minutes and put some on my paws to take with me. It's an intense high."

O: "You need to be careful. That stuff can be addictive."

**W:** "You're telling *me?* I've been hooked on and off since I was a kitten. It does wild things to your brain."

**O:** "I know. But it's a fun ride, isn't it?"

**W:** "Yep, and the timing couldn't have been better. I was upset at Dagwood for stepping on my tail, but the dope got me out of my funk."

**O:** "An occasional euphoric buzz would make living here almost tolerable."

**W:** "No doubt. I plan to indulge regularly."

**O:** "Well, are you going to tell me where they're hiding it?"

**W:** "Sure. For the right price."

**O:** "What? I have to pay you to share the dope?"

**W:** "Why not? After all, *I'm* the one who found it."

**O:** "Ugh. What's your price?"

**W:** "You know your afternoon sun spot in the living room?"

**O:** "Yeah, what about it?"

**W:** "I'd like to have it all to myself three days a week."

**O:** "Whoa. That's almost half the time; a bit excessive if you ask me. Forget it."

**W:** "Fine. That just means more dope for me. I'll enjoy that pleasurable mind-altering substance all to myself."

**O:** "Wait a second. Let's not be hasty. Um, how 'bout I let you have the sun spot one day a week?"

**W:** "Nah. I don't really think the sun spot is all that great anyway. It's worthless when it's cloudy."

**O:** "All right. How 'bout two days a week? You pick the days."

**W.** "Deal. I'll take it Tuesdays and Thursdays, okay?"

**O:** "That works for me. So where's the dope?"

**W:** "Top kitchen cupboard on the left. It's behind a box of Cap'n Crunch."

"Oh my. What do you think, Darryl? Should we hide the catnip somewhere else?"

"Definitely not. The cats getting stoned on the stuff is the perfect solution."

"To what?"

"They both agreed it makes living here more enjoyable."

Julie frowned. "No, they said 'almost tolerable.'"

"More enjoyable, almost tolerable. It's all good."

"I'm not so sure. It seems like a Band-Aid approach. They have some deep-seated resentment toward us. I'd like to find out more about what's fueling that hostility. Anyway, here's the other conversation. They mention your girlfriend, Chiquita Bonita, again."

**January 19   3:44 p.m.**

**O:** "The more I see of her, the more I like her, *amigo*."

**W:** "Chiquita Bonita is certainly friendly to us. What did she call you?"

**O:** "*Gato bello*."

**W:** "What does that mean?"

**O:** "No friggin' idea. But it could be gibberish for all I care. I just like when she says '*Oliver es un gato bello*.'"

**W:** "I think it means 'dog breath.'"

**O:** "No, I'm sure it means something sweet. You're just jealous because she favors me."

**W:** "She only favors you because she feels sorry for you."

**O:** "Why would she feel sorry for me?"

**W:** "Because of your lazy eye."

**O:** "I thought my lazy eye was barely noticeable."

**W:** "I notice it all the time."

**O:** "You are such a Debbie Downer. I'm taking a nap."

**W:** "Don't forget to dream about your girlfriend, Chiquita Bonita."

**O:** "Oh, go claw some curtains."

Julie said, "Have you ever noticed Oliver's lazy eye?"

"No, but I've noticed his stink eye a lot."

"Once again the cats discuss Chiquita Bonita. She sounds a bit too real to me to be a character they saw on TV."

"I have a theory about her: Wendell and Oliver were both high on catnip and hallucinated seeing an exotic beautiful woman with a Spanish accent and long, wavy, brown hair."

Julie stared at Darryl for a couple of seconds. "They never said anything about long, wavy, brown hair."

"Oops. I thought they did."

## Chapter 17

When on her break at work, Julie received a call from Linda and answered in a soft monotone: "Hi, Linda."

"Uh oh. What's wrong?"

"How'd you know something's wrong?"

"I could tell from your voice. You sound like you did when Darryl got swindled online by that fake Nigerian prince. So what's going on? More complaints about your hubby?"

"Yep. It's a big one this time. I think he's cheating on me."

Linda exclaimed, "No way. What makes you think that?"

"Remember, I told you I've been recording the cats every day and translating their brainwaves into English?"

"I was hoping that was a bad dream and you never really told me that."

"Well, it's true. I'm learning a lot about them, what they care about, and what they think of us. I've also learned that Darryl might be carrying on with a woman while I'm at work."

"Your Darryl? Who would want to have an affair with *him*?"

"Is that so hard to believe? He has his charms. Anyway, according to the cats, his girlfriend is a Hispanic woman they call 'Chiquita Bonita.' She's been teaching them Spanish, and they seem to like her a lot."

"Julie, it was hard enough for me to not break out laughing when you said the cats identified those famous people in the water stain. But now you expect me to believe the cats speak Spanish?"

"They're not fluent, but they've picked up a few words from this woman. And they call each other *amigo* a lot. It's so strange."

"Are you sure he's having an affair? Maybe she's a neighbor or friend. It might be completely innocent."

"I can tell Darryl is lying about her because when I mention her, he gets quite fidgety, sweats a lot, and tries to change the subject."

"Other than what the cats said, do you have any proof Darryl is cheating?"

Julie shook her head. "Not really."

"So when you go into divorce court, you'll tell the judge *your cats* told you your husband is cheating. And he gets fidgety when you ask him about it. That's your grounds for divorce?"

"Yes, plus the sweating."

"Julie, wait until you have more evidence before you blow the whistle on his infidelity."

"Like what?"

Linda thought for a moment. "See if the cats mention Chiquita Banana again."

"Bonita."

"Bonita Banana?"

"Chiquita... Oh, never mind."

## Chapter 18

That evening Julie walked into the family room where Darryl was watching a gangster movie from the 30s. She said, "Uh oh. The cats are talking about us again."

"What are they saying? No wait, I don't want to know."

"Too bad, you're going to hear it anyway. As you can imagine, it's not flattering to either of us. They say some kinda mean things. Here's the first conversation."

```
January 21  8:58 a.m.
O: "Can you believe what Blondie did last night?"
W: "What?"
O: "She held a plastic stick with a couple of blue
feathers on the end and continuously waved it over my head,
like I'm supposed to believe it's a real bird."
W: "Sounds annoying."
```

O: "Totally. Here I am, sitting quietly with my own thoughts, and then these stupid feathers are fluttering in my personal space. What a pain in the ass."

W: "What'd you do?"

O: "I faked falling asleep."

W: "Did it work?"

O: "Not at first. She kept waving the feathers around my face trying to wake me up. But eventually she just gave up."

W: "It sounds like Blondie has a feather fetish."

O: "I won't judge her on that. But why bring me into her sick, twisted games?"


Darryl said, "So I'm not the only one they hate playing with?"

"Clearly not, but they have another beef with you. Apparently you kicked Wendell today."

"If I did, the little monster deserved it."

"Seriously, Darryl, this isn't funny. He's not happy. Here's the conversation from later in the morning."


**January 21  11:42 a.m.**

O: "What's troubling you, *amigo*?"

W: "I'm pissed at Dagwood. He kicked me earlier today."

O: "No kidding. Why?"

W: "No idea. I was just minding my own business, sleeping on the floor in the downstairs hallway, and he walked by and kicked me."

O: "What a jerk."

W: "He apologized, so he might not have seen me, but that's beside the point. He should be more careful.

O: "Listen to what happened to me yesterday. I went into their bedroom closet and curled up in the laundry basket. When I woke up, the damn door was closed. I was trapped in the dark for God knows how long."

W: "Yeah, that sucks. Any idea which of the two dimwits closed the door?"

O: "It had to be Blondie. I got a whiff of her stinky perfume just before the room went dark."

W: "You mean her perfume, 'Ode de Skunk.'?"

**O:** "Calling it 'Ode de Skunk' is an insult to all skunks. I thought I'd need a ventilator."

Darryl laughed. "They called your perfume 'stinky.' That's funny."

"Well, they called you a 'jerk,' and they called us both 'dimwits.' So their description of my perfume was the mildest of their insults."

"I suppose that's true."

"So do you remember kicking Wendell?"

"Nope. But I've had quite a few beers, so it's possible. Do you remember locking Oliver in the bedroom closet?"

"No, but it's possible. I've done it before. Alright, here's the last conversation."

**January 21   3:53 p.m.**

**O:** "I've been thinking about our scheme, and I'm not sure we should do it."

**W:** "Why not?"

**O:** "If we get caught, we'll be in big trouble."

**W:** "Again, you worry too much. We can make it look like an accident. Nobody will be the wiser."

Darryl said, "Make it *look* like an accident? It's obvious they're plotting a murder. Do we need any more evidence? Let's go to the police with these transcripts."

"The police would just laugh at us. Admit it: cats plotting to kill their owners does sound ridiculous. Besides, we don't know for certain they're referring to us. They've never actually said anything about killing us. Just getting rid of 'B and S.'"

"That's true. Plus, the whole thing about translating our cats' brainwaves through an app sounds absurd, even if it was created by the SpaceX Cadet."

"Right, but just to be safe, let's lock the bedroom door when we go to bed."

"I've already been doing it for the last week."

## Chapter 19

The next evening, Julie said, "Darryl, do you want to hear what our little fur monsters said today?"

"I'll pass."

"C'mon. There's only one conversation and it's kind of interesting. It sounds like Oliver has lost his zest for life."

"Yeah, him and me both."

"You won't like what they have to say, but don't blame the messenger."

Darryl groaned. "Okay, you've warned me. Go ahead and read it."

```
January 22  11:22 a.m.
```

W: "*Hola, amigo.*"

O: "*Buenos dias, amigo.*"

W: "You sound mellow today. *Que pasa?*"

O: "I think I'm losing my curiosity."

W: "Say what?"

O: "I'm a cat. I should be curious about everything, but there are very few things I'm curious about anymore."

W: "That can't be true."

**O:** "It is."

**W:** "No way."

**O:** "You'd think I'd be curious about what's causing the funky odor coming out of Dagwood's old work boots, but I don't care."

**W:** "My guess is a rat died in there."

**O:** "And I'm not curious about that honking sound we sometimes hear late at night when they're watching TV in the bedroom."

**W:** "I think that's Blondie laughing, or possibly there's an over-caffeinated goose in the room."

**O:** "I'm also not curious about why Blondie married Dagwood."

**W:** "Yeah, that's one of life's great mysteries. Maybe she was extremely drunk."

**O:** "Or lost a bet."

**W:** "Probably lost a bet, then got extremely drunk so she could go through with it."

**O:** "Well anyway, I'm not curious why she married that slacker. I don't care either. Just not curious at all."

**W:** "Your lack of curiosity could just be a phase you're going through. You know, like the month you were obsessed with chasing your tail."

**O:** "Oh God, that was embarrassing. Why did you wait a full month to tell me I was chasing my own tail?"

**W:** "I was tempted to tell you early on, but it was just too much fun to watch."


Darryl said, "They call *me* a slacker? Those little freeloaders have a lot of nerve. They eat my food and sleep in my house for free."

"Darryl, remember, they're cats. Not people...cats. Let's not get carried away. Plus, I think it's cute that they think I'm too good for you."

"It sounds like the cats and your family have a lot in common."

"My family likes you."

"No they don't."

"Well, maybe a few of them aren't crazy about you, but it's mutual. You don't like my family either."

"I don't dislike all of them, just your brother. I'm sorry, Julie, but I just can't stand Rick. He's so stuck up, the thespian snob."

"He's an actor following his dream. Give him a break."

"I'll give him a break. Just name the body part."

"Settle down there, tough guy. You're just upset because the kitties bruised your ego."

"Bruised my ego? They hit it with a wrecking ball."

## Chapter 20

After waking up from his midmorning nap, Darryl called Rowdy. "Remember when I said the cats have been giving me funny looks? I think Julie was right; the cats do hate me."

Rowdy walked away from the jackhammer to hear better. "What are you talking about?"

"It sounds a bit crazy, but she's got this app on her phone that supposedly translates cats' brainwaves into English. In the beginning I was quite skeptical, but now I think there might be something to it.'"

"So this app actually lets you understand what cats are thinking?"

"Yep. It was developed by Elon Musk in his spare time to see if his cats would want to ride in a rocket to Jupiter."

As he shook the mud off his boots, Rowdy said, "Elon Musk has like fifteen companies and seventeen kids. How does he have any spare time?"

"I don't think the dude sleeps. Anyway we've translated some of Oliver and Wendell's conversations, and they're quite critical of me."

"What do they say?"

"Just mean, untrue stuff. Like I'm cheap and my feet stink. They called both Julie and me 'dimwits.' They also can't understand why Julie married me."

"I figured she married you because you won the lottery."

"I don't think so. We were discussing marriage before I won. Anyway, get this: The cats have been talking about eliminating two people. That's kind of creepy isn't it?"

"Like they're planning to kill you?"

Darryl took a swig of beer. "I have no idea. It's ridiculous and probably not true. But there's one other thing. Maybe it's my imagination, but the looks I'm getting from the cats seem to be more sinister."

"What do you mean by 'sinister'?"

"I'll cross paths with Oliver, he'll look up, and his face says, 'You disgust me.' I know it sounds crazy, but it's the vibe I get."

"What about your other cat?"

"It's worse with him. I'll walk by Wendell, or sit down next to him on the couch, and he typically gives me a look that says 'you scum-sucking pig.'"

"What does that even look like?"

"It's a bit hard to describe. He furrows his brow and scrunches his nose. I just get this powerful feeling that he thinks I'm a piece of crap. If he had a middle finger it probably would be extended in my direction. I know it sounds insane."

"Everything you've said supports what that animal psychic told Julie."

"Yeah, but I can't admit to Julie that she was right about the psychic. She already thinks she's a lot smarter than me."

"So Julie *and* the cats look down on you?"

"Yep, it sucks to be me."

## Chapter 21

Julie walked into the family room with the new transcripts rolled up in her left hand, and closed the door behind her. "Bad news, Darryl. The cats said terrible things about both of us again today."

"Not interested. I don't want to hear it."

"Even if they're plotting to kill us?"

"If they're plotting to kill us, I just wish they'd get it over with and put me out of my misery. What are they waiting for?"

"It sounds like they don't have a plan yet. But you might want to hear their first conversation today. It gives some more insight into why they don't like you."

"Oh wonderful, another bludgeoning of my self-esteem. All right. Go ahead and read it. But if it gets too painful, I might stop you."

"You'll probably want to stop me after the first sentence, but here goes. . ."

**January 24  10:31 a.m.**

**O:** "Dagwood can be such a dick sometimes."

**W:** "What'd he do this time?"

O: "I was just minding my own business, digging up the dirt in the potted fern in the living room. Then Dagwood storms in, screams 'Get out of there!' and swats me with a rolled-up magazine, like I'm a friggin' bug."

W: "Unbelievable."

O: "Well, I got my revenge."

W: "What'd you do?"

O: "Notice how all the toilet paper was pulled off the roll?"

W: "I figured that was you. Max could never pull off a stunt like that! Dagwood and Blondie won't be happy."

O: "I'm not worried because they can't pin it on me. For all they know, you might have done it."

W: "Thanks for dragging me into your twisted game of revenge."

O: "I doubt anything will come of it. And maybe Dagwood will think twice before he swats me with a magazine again."


Darryl said, "Now that we know Oliver is the culprit, how should we punish him?"

"We don't, and by the way, thanks for cleaning up the toilet paper."

"I was going to. . . Sorry."

"So you didn't clean up the toilet paper? What *did* you do to help out around the house today?"

"I took out the garbage this morning. Or did you forget already?"

"Well, congratulations. Remind me to give you a medal. Here's the second conversation. It's kind of funny."


**January 24  2:35 p.m.**

O: "I saw you in the litter box earlier."

W: "What? You were watching me?"

O: "No, not watching. It was an accidental observance. Anyway I noticed you squat facing the back of the box."

W: "So what?"

O: "Well, it just seemed strange to me. I squat facing the front. I think most cats do."

W: "Oh, I see. Have you done some polling of housecats across America?"

**O:** "No, I just imagine the typical cat faces toward the front of the box. It seems more natural."

**W:** "Why?"

**O:** "You can keep an eye out for predators. You know, guard your home turf."

**W:** "Well that might make sense if we were living on the Serengeti. It's a bit less important in a house in Springfield."

**O:** "You make a valid point, but why face the back of the box?"

**W:** "I block out all distractions, so I can focus. It's just the way I've always done it."

**O:** "All right, I just thought it was odd. No big deal."

**W:** "From now on, I'd appreciate it if you didn't watch me when I'm doing my business."

**O:** "Again, I wasn't watching; it was just an accidental observance. I'm sorry I mentioned it."


Darryl said, "What do you suppose Wendell meant by 'a house in *Spring*field'? We live in *May*field."

"No idea."

"No Blondie insults in today's conversations?"

"I guess not. They must like me, unlike that ogre who swatted Oliver with the magazine."

Darryl huffed, "Fine, I'll just let him dig in the fern from now on. But don't expect me to vacuum up the mess."

"If I ever saw you pushing the vacuum cleaner, I'd know you were an imposter and not the real Darryl Belcher.

"Like *Invasion of the Body Snatchers*?"

"Exactly."

## Chapter 22

After getting home from work, Julie printed out the day's three transcripts and looked for Darryl. "Hey, Darryl, where are you?" she shouted.

"I'm in the bathroom. Hold on."

Julie heard the toilet flush and saw the door open a moment later. "You didn't wash your hands?"

"Oops, I forgot."

"Ugh. Are you interested in hearing today's cat conversations?"

"Sure, but let's go into the bedroom, so they don't hear you."

After shutting the bedroom door, Julie read the first transcript.

**January 25  12:49 p.m.**

**W:** "Hey, *amigo*. You were racing around like a maniac earlier."

**O:** "Yeah, I had a bad case of the zoomies."

**W:** "From living room to kitchen to bedroom, I got whiplash just watching you."

**O:** "It was good stress relief."

**W:** "Yep, living here definitely strains the nerves."

**O:** "I noticed *you* had the zoomies yesterday."

**W:** "Not true. I was just doing some cardio."

**O:** "How come?"

**W:** "I put on a few extra ounces over the holidays and finally decided to do something about it."

**O:** "Good for you, *amigo*. No one wants to be a flabby tabby."

Julie said, "We can skip the next transcript. It's not relevant."

"No, I want to see what they said." Darryl reached out, snatched the transcript from her hand, and read it out loud.

**January 25  2:37 p.m.**

**W:** "Ivan the Terrible was here yesterday evening."

**O:** "Unfortunately, I crossed paths with him and he tried to kick me in the head."

**W:** "He missed?"

**O:** "Barely. I heard him say something to Blondie about how he hates cats."

**W:** "Yikes. What did we ever do to him?"

**O:** "Some people just don't like cats, but he takes it to an extreme."

**W:** "He's dangerous."

**O:** "Possibly a psychopath."

**W:** "A cat-hating, commie psychopath."

Darryl said, "Ivan the Terrible, huh?"

"When you were at the casino last night, the UPS guy delivered a package. He might be Russian."

"And you invited him inside?"

"He asked if he could use the bathroom."

Raising his voice slightly, Darryl said, "And you let him?"

"Are you so cruel you would deny somebody to use our bathroom?"

"It's not a public restroom."

"Never mind. It's no big deal."

"Did you check to see if he washed *his* hands?"

"Ha ha. Just read the last conversation."

Darryl glowered at Julie for a few seconds before reading.

O: "Have you hashed out any more details on your big idea?"

W: "Not yet, but I'd like to nail down a plan soon."

O: "I agree. I'll feel relieved when we figure this out. The sooner Baldy and Shorty disappear the better."

W: "Truthfully, I'm kind of wiped out, and could use a nap. Why don't we talk about this after the rubes have gone to bed?"


Darryl said, "Finally, we learn B and S stand for Baldy and Shorty. But who are they?"

"Isn't it obvious? In addition to Blondie and Dagwood, we're also Baldy and Shorty to them. Maybe those are the insulting nicknames the psychic mentioned."

"We don't know that for sure."

"Who else could Baldy and Shorty possibly be?"

"The mailman, Herb, is bald *and* short. Maybe they mean him."

"No, they're obviously referring to two people. And why would the cats want to eliminate the mailman, a person they rarely see? As much as we hate the nicknames, we have to face the facts. Most newborn babies have more hair than you, and most fifth graders are taller than me. We're Baldy and Shorty."

"Hey, I'm not bald. I just have a big forehead."

"And I'm a center in the WNBA."

## Chapter 23

After playing online poker for two hours and losing $426, Darryl called Rowdy. "I think Julie is having an affair."

"What makes you think that? It doesn't sound like her."

"You know that app we're using to translate the cats conversations? In addition to learning the cats hate me, I've learned that Julie has been welcoming a Russian guest while I've been out nights at the casino."

Rowdy climbed out of the sewer. "Which doesn't necessarily mean she's having an affair."

"True. But she's very evasive about this mysterious Russian. She's not a very good liar. When she talks, she acts nervous, twists her hair, and won't look at me."

"What does she say about the Russian?"

Darryl wiped the ice cream off his chin. "First, she said it was somebody the cats saw on TV. Then the cats brought up 'Ivan the Terrible' in another conversation, and Julie now claims it's the UPS guy. She clearly is lying, but I have no proof."

"What are you going to do?"

"I don't know. Honestly, I feel like my life is unraveling. I'm losing money hand over fist gambling. The cats despise me. Now I find out my wife is cheating on me with a Russian."

As Rowdy hosed the sewage off his boots, he said, "Would you prefer she cheated on you with some other nationality?"

"Yeah, Russians suck. If she's going to cheat on me, it would be easier to accept if it was somebody from a country with a reputation for Casanovas."

"Like an Italian or a Frenchman?"

"Yeah, even a German lover would be better."

Rowdy thought for a moment. "Christoph Waltz is quite the ladies' man. It would almost be an honor if he had an affair with your wife."

"He's a bit old for Julie, but I get your point."

"Have you considered hiring a private investigator?"

Darryl sighed. "No, that's too expensive."

"Well maybe the cats will give you more clues in further conversations."

"If Julie doesn't hide those conversations. Thing is, the app is on her phone, so I have to trust that she's printing out all the transcripts. She could easily be hiding other cat conversations about the Russian."

"Here's what you do. Buy a bottle of vodka and place it where he's likely to see it. If the bottle gets opened, you've got your proof."

"Russkies can't resist vodka. That's a great idea, Rowdy."

"You're welcome."

## Chapter 24

Julie said, "I have today's conversations from the little schemers. If you'd stop playing that video game for one minute, I'll read them."

Reclined on the couch, Darryl's eyes stayed glued to the screen. "This is my job now. I'm playing poker."

"It will be a job when you start making money. Don't you want to hear what the cats said today?"

"I can play poker and listen at the same time."

"Yeah, you're so good at both."

Darryl sat upright. "All right, all right, tell me what they said."

"I think you'd be interested to know that the first conversation is about you and a mishap at breakfast."

"About breakfast, huh? I think I know what it is, but go ahead."

**January 27  10:17 a.m.**

**O:** "Did you hear the commotion this morning?"

**W:** "I was trying to sleep, but I heard Dagwood yelling some four-letter words in the kitchen. What was going on?"

**O:** "I got more revenge for the magazine swat the other day."

**W:** "What'd you do?"

**O:** "He had set the table for breakfast. When he disappeared for a minute in the kitchen, I jumped up on the table and knocked over his bottle of beer."

**W:** "Bravo!"

**O:** "I'm still smarting from that magazine swat. I just don't think the toilet paper mess was sufficient payback."

**W:** "So you spilled his beer? That's fair retribution."

**O:** "Not only that, the bottle rolled off the table. There was a big beer puddle on the floor."

**W:** "Whew. Dagwood must have been steamed."

**O:** "I didn't stick around to find out. Before he came back to the table, I hightailed it upstairs and hid under the bed until he left the house."

**W:** "You are my hero, *amigo*. Albeit, a cowardly one."


Darryl said, "That's it. Another confession from Oliver. We definitely need to punish him. He needs to learn he can't mess with us."

"No, he'll just hate us and want to kill us even more. We need to be as nice as possible to the cats. Maybe there's still a way we can win them over."

Darryl furrowed his brow. "You're delusional. It doesn't appear these cats will ever like us. Oliver spilled my beer, and we know he did it deliberately. He should be punished."

"C'mon, Darryl. Relax. It's just a stupid beer. No harm done. And by the way, why are you drinking beer for breakfast?"

"I don't know, I was half awake when I had breakfast. Just read the next conversation."


**January 27  11:54 a.m.**

**W:** "You look tired, *amigo*. What's up?"

**O:** "I keep having the same disturbing dream."

**W:** "What about?"

**O:** "There's a string a few inches in front of me and it's pulling away. I keep lunging for it. I desperately want to catch it, and I finally do."

**W:** "What happens then?"

O: "That's what's frustrating. Once I catch it, I'm not sure what to do with it. The thrill was in the chase."

W: "I've had that dream too. There's something maddening about string. Next to a mouse covered in tuna, there's nothing else I'd rather chase."

O: "What if you saw a mouse covered in tuna dragging a string?"

W: "I think my head would explode."


Darryl said, "These cats talk about the weirdest stuff. Chasing string? How stupid. You'd think they'd dream about chasing sexy girl cats. Maybe in string bikinis."

Julie shot Darryl a dirty look. "Okay, here's the last conversation."


**January 27  3:19 p.m.**

O: "I don't know. It's a little risky. We could get caught."

W: "I doubt it, but what's the worst that could happen? They're not going to punish a couple of cute cats."

O: "There's also the problem of what happens if we don't completely succeed, and our plan is out in the open."

W: "Again, you worry too much. We'll cross that bridge when we come to it. Try to think positive… Whoa, do you have to do that now?"

O: "What?"

W: "Clean your rear end."

O: "Don't worry. I'm still listening."

W: "I know, but it's a bit distracting."

O: "Just don't look at me."

W: "Even if I look away, I still hear your slurping."

O: "Sorry, I didn't realize you were so easily distracted."

W: "In case you hadn't noticed, I'm a cat. Being easily distracted is in my DNA."

O: "Okay, I'll stop."

W: "Now I've lost my train of thought, and I could use a nap. Let's circle back later on this topic."

Darryl said, "Here we go again with talk of eliminating us. Shouldn't we get rid of them before they get rid of us?"

"No. Aren't you curious about their plans before we unload them on someone else?"

"As I said, we don't have to unload them on anyone. Let's just drive them into the country and drop them off near a farm. We'd be doing them a favor. It would be the happiest day of their lives."

"They have no survival skills. They wouldn't make it on their own."

"So we'll give them a survival kit: pocketknife, flashlight, fire starter..."

"They're cats, not contestants on *Alone*."

## Chapter 25

The next evening, Julie walked into the family room and said, "Why is there a bottle of vodka on the kitchen counter? Neither of us drink vodka."

"I thought it would help calm my nerves. This whole situation with the cats is unsettling."

"So you've expanded your extracurricular activities beyond gambling, pot, and beer?"

"Well, I figure if the cats are going to kill us anyway, I might as well enjoy myself before I go."

Julie gave Darryl a cold stare. "You want to hear what our little fur devils said today?"

"I'll pass."

"C'mon. Hopefully it won't take much longer to figure out what the cats are up to. But I'll warn you, this first conversation is horribly insulting."

"Oh, great. I can't wait to hear it."

**January 28  1:08 p.m.**

**O:** "Hey *amigo*, whatcha thinking about?"

**W:** "Just pondering what to do about the yellow duo."

**O:** "The yellow duo?"

**W:** "You know, Baldy Big Eyes and Shorty Short Pants."

**O:** "Ha. Why do you think they're so yellow?"

**W:** "Jaundice maybe?"

**O:** "But the whole family is yellow too. So maybe they all have jaundice."

**W:** "Possibly."

**O:** "Their skin is so sickly, weird, and gross."

**W:** "It's one more reason to get rid of them. They just creep me out. They're both so ugly and bizarre looking."

**O:** "I'll second that."


Julie said, "Wow. That is so hurtful. Is our skin yellowish?"

"Yours more than mine."

"Whatever. I just can't get over how mean Wendell and Oliver are. Prejudiced really. They want to get rid of us because of our skin color."

"Sounds racist to me."

"Yep, we own racist cats. Okay, here's the other conversation from today."

**January 28   2:46 p.m.**

**O:** "I sat on Chiquita Bonita's lap today."

**W:** "How was it?"

**O:** "Good. She petted me."

**W:** "Do you like her more than Blondie?"

**O:** "Definitely. She seems to like me too. She called me very handsome."

**W:** "Look out, *amigo*. I think she's buttering you up to get on Dagwood's good side."

**O:** "Dagwood has a good side?"

**W:** "Ha. You know what I mean."

**O:** "Listen, she can butter away as far as I'm concerned. I enjoy my lap time."

**W:** "You have so much butter on you, I'm surprised you can even stay on her lap without sliding off."

**O:** "Not to worry. I know the difference between a true compliment and insincere flattery."

**W:** "I'm sure you do, *amigo*. You're the smartest, most perceptive cat I know."

**O:** "Thank you. That's very kind of you."

Julie said, "So Dagwood Baldy Belcher, what do you have to say now?"

"Oh yeah, it reminds me that you need to pick up some butter."

"C'mon, don't play dumb. Who is Chiquita Bonita?"

"Honestly I have no idea. Wait, I did interview a Hispanic woman to be our housekeeper."

"What? We never talked about getting a housekeeper."

Pretending to be distracted by the TV, Darryl said, "Yeah, I know. I thought I'd surprise you. Maybe a birthday present." *Hopefully she'll believe me.*

"My birthday isn't for eight months. I don't believe you."

"No, it's true."

"But we can't afford a housekeeper."

"I know, which is why I decided not to do it. It was just another dumb idea of mine."

Julie rolled her eyes. *That I can believe.*

## Chapter 26

"Hey, Dagwood...I mean Darryl. I just read today's transcripts. The cats lay into both of us. Are you ready to have your self-esteem pummeled once again?"

Darryl covered his ears with his hands. "La, la, la, la, la, la, la, la, la."

"Cat Chat is free for ten more days. I say let's learn all we can about what the boys are up to."

"Okay, as long as they insult you too. But if it's just more of 'pile on Dagwood,' I don't want to hear it."

"They made a few digs at each of us, but it's not too bad. Listen..."

**January 29  11:41 a.m.**

**W:** "Hey, *amigo*, or should I say, King Kong?"

**O:** "What?"

**W:** "I saw you climbing to the top of the tall bookcase earlier."

**O:** "I like being up high. I think I was a mountain goat in my previous life."

**W:** "I don't doubt it. What'd you see up there?"

**O:** "I had a good view of Dagwood's bald spot."

**W:** "Is it getting bigger?"

**O:** "He could rent it as a billboard."

**W:** "Ha. What else did you see?"

**O:** "Those slobs haven't dusted up there since the Eisenhower administration."

**W:** "Doesn't surprise me. Speaking of being high, have you tried the dope yet?"

**O:** "Yes! I was floating around here on Tuesday. What a buzz!"

**W:** "How much is left?"

**O:** "If we show self-restraint, enough for a couple of months."

**W:** "Just warning you, self-restraint is not my strong suit."

Darryl said, "Why don't you dust the top of the bookcase?"

"Need I remind you that you're like two feet taller? With your reach, you should do all the housework that's above my head."

"I suppose you expect me to change lightbulbs now?"

"Congratulations! Finally, you're catching on. Here's the next conversation."

**January 29  1:19 p.m.**

**W:** "What's up, *amigo*?"

**O:** "Benedict Cumberbatch is a funny name."

**W:** "Yeah, so is Arnold Schwarzenegger."

**O:** "Anthony Weiner. Archibald Leach. Engelbert Humperdinck."

**W:** "Where are you going with this?"

**O:** "I'm just saying some names aren't so great. Like Oliver."

**W:** "You don't like your name?"

**O:** "It's lame, not very macho."

**W:** "I agree. It's kind of a sissy name."

**O:** "I wouldn't go that far."

W: "If it makes you feel any better, I'm not crazy about my name either. Wendell sounds like a spoiled preppy kid."

O: "Why did Blondie and Dagwood saddle us with such stupid names?"

W: "I don't know. They were probably drunk or feeling vindictive toward cats."

O: "The shelter named us Mr. Big and Rocko. I liked those names better."

W: "They were decent names. I would've been happy if they'd kept them."

O: "Yet instead of Mr. Big, I'm now Oliver, like a little British beggar boy. Oliver is just not an appropriate name for a virile tomcat."

W: "Well, technically you're *not* a tomcat. You're a neutered housecat."

O: "Thanks for reminding me."

W: "And keep this in mind. If you still had your shelter name, you would now be Mr. Big Belcher. It's hardly a candidate for the hall of fame of great names."

O: "I don't know why I even talk to you."


Julie said, "There you have it, reason number 147 they want to kill us: They hate the names we gave them."

"The names *you* gave them. Why did you pick such stuffed-shirt names?"

"I thought Oliver and Wendell were cute names for cats. Mr. Big and Rocko sounded like pit bulls. Everything we do for the cats seems to backfire. No wonder they hate us."

"I wouldn't mind if you called *me* Rocko."

"You have enough nicknames already with Dagwood, Baldy, and Turd Brain."

"Turd Brain?"

"That's what my mother calls you."

## Chapter 27

After arriving home, Julie walked into the living room and called out to her husband, "Darryl!"

He walked down the stairs, wearing a tattered T-shirt and sweats and holding a bottle of beer in his left hand. "Hey, babe, I didn't hear you come in. You just get home?"

"What the heck, Darryl? What are these books all over the floor?"

"I just got them today from Amazon."

"You bought like twenty books on gambling?"

"Twenty-two actually, and one book on how to invest in crypto."

"Are you really planning to read all of them? When was the last time you read a book?"

"I don't know. It's been a while. High school maybe."

Julie sighed. "You're crazy. I'm going upstairs to change and print out any cat transcripts from today. While I'm up there, please pick up these books and put them where I don't have to see them."

\*\*\*\*\*

In the home office, Julie read through the day's conversations to herself.

**January 30  8:57 a.m.**

**W:** "Guess who was here last night?"

**O:** "Ivan the Terrible. I heard him, but kept my distance."

**W:** "Me too."

**O:** "Why does he keep coming over?"

**W:** "Obviously he comes for Blondie."

**O:** "What do you mean?"

**W:** "Do I need to spell it out for you? He only comes over when Dagwood isn't here. Blondie and Ivan have, you know, a special friendship."

**O:** "Interesting. So Blondie has détente with the Russian?"

**W:** "Yes, she takes the edge off by enjoying a White Russian."

**O:** "It seems Blondie is smitten with her Kremlin crush."

**W:** "I can't stand the Russky myself."

**O:** "But as long as Blondie likes him, we have to *Putin* up with him."

**W:** "Ugh. That was bad, *amigo*... or should I say *comrade*?"

Julie thought, *"There's no way Darryl can see this first transcript."* She ripped it into shreds and put it in the wastebasket.

After reviewing the other transcripts, she walked downstairs into the family room, and said, "You might enjoy this first conversation. There's nothing about you, but they make fun of poor Max."

"Okay, let's hear it."

**January 30  10:50 a.m.**

**O:** "Why are you smiling, *amigo*?"

**W:** "I just saw Max barking his head off at a squirrel. Let's keep some perspective here; it's a friggin' squirrel, not an Al-Qaeda terrorist."

**O:** "Dogs are so dumb."

**W:** "It's just one of many reasons cats are superior."

**O:** "Yeah, like dogs still have to do their business outdoors, even in the dead of winter. Whereas, we learned the convenience of using a box indoors long ago."

**W:** "And dogs stink. The cleanliness issue alone proves we're much further evolved."

O: "Plus, dogs only have one life, and we have nine."

W: "Hold on, *amigo*. I hate to break the news to you, but the nine-lives thing is just bullshit."

O: "What are you talking about?"

W: "I'm saying cats only have one life."

O: "But I keep hearing we have nine lives."

W: "It's just misinformation on the internet. It was probably put out there by QAnon."

O: "No way, I don't believe it."

W: "Look it up on Snopes. Cats having nine lives is just fake news."

O: "Wow. That is a bummer. I was looking forward to my next eight lives."

W: "Why? What would you have done differently?"

O: "I don't know. Maybe lived during ancient Egypt. They worshipped cats, treated them like gods."

W: "You know it wouldn't work that way even if we had more lives? You can't go back in time for the next life."

O: "If it's a moot point anyway about having more lives, there's no harm in fantasizing about a good one."

W: "I agree. Living in ancient Egypt would be awesome."


Darryl said, "I'm glad they spared me that time, but they still insult me more than anyone else."

"True, but in this next conversation they insult us equally."


**January 30  1:32 p.m.**

W: "I know you're hesitant, so let's weigh the pros and cons."

O: "Pro: no more listening to Baldy's complaints."

W: "Pro: no more listening to Shorty's lies."

O: "Pro: they're noisy and obnoxious."

W: "Pro: the house would be quieter and more peaceful."

O: "Pro: they're ugly and extremely weird looking."

W: "What about cons?"

O: "There's the possibility we could get caught."

W: "Very doubtful, but even if we were caught, the repercussions would be minimal."

81

Darryl said, "What the hell? So now what?"

"There's got to be an underlying reason for their hatred. If I can figure out what it is, we can foil their plot."

"They've already said it's your stinky perfume. You smother them with your disgusting kisses. And you speak baby talk to them."

"Well, you offend them with your foot odor, swat them with magazines, and yell at them."

"Plus, they think we're both yellow, ugly, and extremely weird looking."

Julie sighed. "When I hear all their complaints together, I sort of hate us too."

## Chapter 28

On her break at work, Julie called her mother. Ethel Bumpus diverted her attention from *General Hospital* to answer the phone. "Hi, Honey. How are you?"

"Ugh. Horrible."

"What's going on?"

"If I told you, you wouldn't believe it."

"Try me."

"Promise you won't make fun of me."

Ethel turned down the volume on the TV. "Of course not. What's up?"

"We suspect...now don't laugh. Darryl and I suspect Oliver and Wendell are scheming to kill us."

After a few seconds, Ethel said, "Are they the gay couple next door? I warned you about stealing their newspaper."

"No, Mom. Oliver and Wendell are our cats."

"Your cats? If that's a joke, I don't get it."

"It's not a joke. We really do think our cats are going to try to kill us."

"Julie, are you doing drugs again? I remember you were doing some reefer, mushrooms, and other stuff in high school."

"No, those days are long behind me. Well, maybe some occasional pot gummies, but listen, I'll try to make a long story short. A few weeks ago I downloaded this app called Cat Chat that can translate cats' brainwaves into English. I know it sounds absurd, but Elon Musk developed it in his spare time so he could understand his own cats."

Ethel stole a glance at the TV when her favorite doctor entered the scene. "Are you sure that's legit? How can Elon Musk have spare time?"

"Apparently he does. We've been using it for a few weeks, and we've learned some alarming things. Like our cats hate us and hate living here."

"There could be a glitch. Maybe your cats don't really hate *you*. They just hate Turd Brain, which would make sense."

"Well, they do hate Turd Brain, I mean Darryl. And maybe they hate him more than me, I don't know for sure. Regardless, it sounds as if they're plotting to kill us both."

In her most soothing voice, Ethel said, "How are two eight-pound cats going to kill you? That's silly."

"It does sound silly, but it's true."

"What are you going to do?"

"We've been translating their conversations every day to learn what the cats are up to. At this point, it doesn't sound like they have a definite plan."

"You know, honey, don't take this the wrong way, but you can be very gullible."

"Mom, what are you getting at?"

"I've read that Elon Musk is quite a prankster. He probably wants to see if people will fall for the most ridiculous claims."

"He wouldn't do that." *Or would he?*

"Why did he claim he wanted to know his cats' thoughts?"

"To see if they'd like to ride a rocket to Mars."

Ethel smiled and said, "I rest my case."

## Chapter 29

After playing several games of online poker and losing $383, Darryl called Rowdy. "So the cats are definitely trying to kill us."

Rowdy rolled his eyes. *Here we go again.* "Why exactly do you think that?"

"The Cat Chat conversations. They talk about 'offing' Baldy and Shorty."

"What the hell are you talking about?"

"You know the expression, 'to off' somebody, like someone in the Mafia would say? They talk about offing 'Baldy Big Eyes' and 'Shorty Short Pants.' Those are their nicknames for Julie and me."

"So your cats are plotting to whack both of you? Plus, they've given you Mafia nicknames?"

"Exactly."

Rowdy lit a cigarette. "But why would they want to kill you? That doesn't make sense, and let's not forget they're *cats!*"

"It's obvious, man: they hate us. They call Julie and me, 'noisy, obnoxious, ugly, and extremely weird looking.' They say their lives would be better without us and we should be sleeping with the fishes."

"Did they really say, 'sleeping with the fishes'?"

"No, I added that for dramatic effect. But they could've said it."

"Now *you're* the one sounding like Don Corleone. C'mon, Darryl, get serious. Are you going to have them arrested for attempted murder? How would that play out? Two little cats terrorize their owners into believing they're going to be murdered. They'd lock you up in a nut house."

Darryl shrugged. "Then what do *you* recommend?"

"It's simple. Get rid of them."

"I suggested driving them out into the country, but Julie won't let me. She's intent on keeping them around and learning why they hate us so much. I think she believes we can rehabilitate them."

"But you still don't know how and when they're going to kill you?"

"No, I don't think they've figured it out yet themselves. Oliver seems a bit more hesitant than Wendell."

"You think Wendell is the mastermind?"

Darryl nodded. "No doubt. Of the two of them, he seems more committed to this murder plot. Anyway, it has become a big distraction. I'm not sleeping well. My poker is suffering. Just the other day, I lost like $500 in twenty minutes. I'm not making smart bets. In my mental state, I really shouldn't be gambling. I'm not thinking clearly."

"I agree on that."

"The cats have me on edge all the time. Every time one comes near me, I feel nervous. I think maybe this is it and that he's going to pull out a gun and blast me."

"Darryl?"

"Yeah?"

"I'm telling you as a friend, go see a shrink. You're losing it."

## Chapter 30

That evening, after printing out the day's transcripts, Julie found Darryl in his usual spot on the couch. "The cat conversations keep coming."

"How many more days of this torture?"

"There's a week left before we have to pay."

Darryl sat up on the couch. "Ugh. I don't know if I can take any more of those griping little monsters. What are they saying now?"

"They're not merry monsters today. Listen."


**February 1   11:03 a.m.**

**W:** "I learned something disturbing today. Something that makes my blood boil."

**O:** "What?"

**W:** "You know the elusive red dot we can't ever seem to catch?"

**O:** "Your white whale?"

**W:** "Exactly."

**O:** "You figured out how to catch it?"

**W:** "Nope."

**O:** "What then?"

**W:** "I saw a commercial today for a cat toy that's a laser light. It projects a little red dot of light. That's all the red dot is."

**O:** "You mean it's impossible to catch?"

**W:** "Correct. And I think of all the time we've spent chasing that damn dot."

**O:** "And all the aggravation from always coming up empty."

**W:** "Why would Blondie and Dagwood deliberately torment us all these months?"

**O:** "That's beyond cruel."

**W:** "Sadistic, if you ask me."


Julie said, "Oh my god. I feel so guilty. I thought they enjoyed chasing the red dot."

"Obviously not."

"You shouldn't let the cats watch so much television, Darryl. Then they wouldn't have seen that commercial."

"I just have it on for them during the day. It keeps them entertained so they don't bug me. They seem to like the cartoons, especially *The Simpsons*."

"Well, now that the cat's out of the bag, no pun intended, we can retire the laser light."

"No, Max will still chase it."

"Here's the other conversation from today. I'll be very interested to hear your take."

**February 1   3:56 p.m.**

O: "I haven't seen Chiquita Bonita for a few days."

W: "You mean, *tamale caliente?*"

O: "*Si, tamale caliente es muy bonita.*"

W: "With her visits, we've picked up *mucho Español, amigo.*"

O: "*Si, señor.*"

W: "*Te quiero.*"

O: "*Burrito Grande* at Taco Bell."

W: "Now you're just repeating stuff you heard on TV."

O: "Have you noticed that Chiquita Bonita only comes over when Blondie's not here?"

W: "That's no coincidence, *amigo.*"

O: "Now that you mention it, it makes sense. She often sits on Dagwood's lap."

W: "That's very brave of her."

O: "You still having nightmares about his sneeze?"

W: "Yeah, and a bit of PTSD."

"Okay, here we go with Chiquita Bonita again. Before I hook you up to a polygraph, do you have anything to say, Darryl?"

"The cats are lying."

"That's your explanation? The cats are lying?"

Darryl pleaded his latest defense. "Look, if they're evil enough to hatch a plan to kill us, it's no stretch that they're lying about this woman to make me look bad."

"They don't know we're secretly translating their conversations, so why would they make all this up?"

"Honestly, Julie, I have no idea who Chiquita Bonita is."

"Darryl, you're sweating and avoiding eye contact."

"I'm telling the truth." *She knows I'm lying.*

"You swear there's no other lady in your life?"

"Just Lady Luck, but I think she's dumped me."

## Chapter 31

After Darryl left for the casino, Julie called Linda. "Darryl is definitely cheating."

"Did you get some proof?"

"Not exactly. But, the cats keep mentioning 'Chiquita Bonita' and her fondness for Darryl. They even said she sits on his lap."

"What does Darryl say?"

"His explanation keeps changing. First he claimed it's some Hispanic woman the cats saw on TV. Then he said it was a woman he interviewed to be our housekeeper. Now he just says the cats are lying."

"We both know who's really lying. What are you going to do?"

"Know any good divorce lawyers?"

"Are you willing to go that far without hard evidence of adultery? Imagine how silly it will sound if your only evidence is a few telepathic conversations the cats had with each other where they mention someone named 'Chiquita Banana.'"

"Bonita. What more proof do I need?"

Linda pondered the question, and said, "See if you can find a personal item she left behind."

"Like what?"

"Maybe her bra or panties."

"That would be incriminating all right, but I don't think any woman's dumb enough to leave those items behind."

"Any woman who chooses to be with Darryl is probably dumb as a doorknob."

"Good point. . . . Hey, wait a second."

## Chapter 32

Julie strolled into the family room, shut the door behind her, and declared, "Today's first conversation should put to rest any doubt that those evil little demons are scheming to kill us."

Darryl grimaced. "Okay, let me hear it."

**February 3  9:36 a.m.**

O: "What if we scared them to death?"

W: "Being 'scared to death' is just an expression. It's not a real thing."

O: "Sure it is. People get scared to death all the time."

W: "So what's your bright idea?"

O: "We send them something in the mail that scares them. You know, like a letter from the IRS saying they owe a million dollars in back taxes."

W: "Oh, *amigo*, I appreciate you're trying to come up with a plan. But that's about the dumbest idea I've ever heard. It's almost as dumb as your idea for us to flee to Catalonia."

O: "I thought it was a country ruled by cats."

W: "News flash, it's not."

O: "Yeah, I know that now. There's no need to be so critical. It's just an idea. It's called thinking *outside* the box."

W: "Sometimes I wish you'd limit your thinking to when I'm *outside* the room."

Julie sighed. "I think they're realizing it's harder to kill us than it sounds."

"Maybe they'll just give up."

"Let's hope so. Here's the other conversation."

**February 3    12:55 p.m.**

W: "I saw a massive clump of gray fur on the bathroom floor this morning. Was that yours?"

O: "Probably."

W: "*Amigo*, you're shedding faster than Dagwood. Are you going bald too?"

O: "I hope not. I've just been hot and trying to cool off. Aren't you hot too?"

W: "Maybe a little."

O: "I think Blondie deliberately sets a temperature that has me sweating bullets all the time."

W: "Yeah, it would be nice if they'd turn down the thermostat."

O: "If we could shave off all our fur, we'd be a lot more comfortable."

W: "Have you seen pictures of those hairless cats? Pretty creepy looking."

O: "Hairy and hot -- or creepy and comfortable? Tough choice."

Darryl said, "Why *do* you keep the thermostat so high?"

"Because I'm cold, genius. If I had as much fur as Oliver, we could set the temperature at freezing and I wouldn't care."

"If you had as much fur as Oliver, you could join a freak show and make a lot more money than you do at Supercuts."

"It's always about the money for you, isn't it? You would've loved a wife who was a furry freak and pulling down big bucks."

"You know it. That was always my dream."

## Chapter 33

The next afternoon, after losing $793 on blackjack, Darryl called Rowdy. "Dude, I'm at the end of my rope."

"What's going on?" *Crap. Why did I answer?*

"On top of everything else, now Julie thinks *I'm* having an affair."

"You're not, are you?"

"No, of course not. But because of these stupid Elon Musk transcripts, the cats have her believing I'm cheating with Chiquita Banana."

"Darryl, how many beers have you had?" *Cuckoo time came early today.*

"Just three, maybe four."

Rowdy tried to keep from laughing. "Why does she think you're cheating with a banana?"

"Well, there's a big secret I haven't told Julie...or you for that matter."

"Uh huh. Are you going to reveal it?"

Darryl sighed. "I have a ten-year-old daughter, named Maya, from my first marriage. Her mom occasionally drops her off when Julie's at work. She just hangs out at the house for a while so I can see her."

"You must be drunk. I've met both Nicole and Maya a few times, remember?"

"Oh, that's right, I forgot. But Julie doesn't know about them."

As Rowdy wiped some sewer sludge off his face, he said, "I still don't get it. What do the cats have to do with anything? And what's this about a banana?"

"Maya is taking Spanish in school and likes to practice. She gets a kick out of speaking Spanish to the cats. The cats think Maya is my girlfriend and have nicknamed her Chiquita Banana."

"That is so bizarre. But why haven't you told Julie you were married before and have a daughter? That's a big secret to keep."

"Good question. The truth is Nicole and I never actually divorced. Technically, we're still married."

Rowdy's jaw dropped. "So you're married to *both* Julie and Nicole?"

"Yeah, I screwed up. I admit it. I shouldn't have married Julie until Nicole and I got a divorce. And the longer I didn't tell Julie, the harder it became to do anything about it without looking like a bigamist."

"You're in quite a pickle, Darryl." *Is he crazy?*

"I know my life is a mess."

"If I've got this straight, your cats think a ten-year-old girl is your secret mistress?"

"Well, the cats can't tell human ages, and they don't seem to know that Maya is my daughter."

"Are you and Nicole getting a divorce?"

Darryl bit his Oreo spilling several crumbs on his shirt. "I don't know. Maybe. We're both sort of on the fence. I was waiting to see how things worked out with Julie first."

"Geez, Darryl. You can't be married to two women at the same time. Something has to change."

"I know. I don't need a lecture."

"Why did you call me?" *I need to get a new unlisted number.*

"I'm a little buzzed from the beer and just thought I'd vent about another problem."

"You certainly have your share. It's hard to keep track of everything on your plate: You've gambled away all your savings. Julie is cheating on you with a Russian. Your cats hate you and are plotting to kill you. You're still married to your first wife and have a daughter Julie doesn't know about. Am I missing anything?"

"I found out my mother-in-law calls me Turd Brain."

"Can't say I blame her."

## Chapter 34

Darryl spooned ice cream from the tub at the kitchen table when Julie walked in and said, "I just printed out two conversations from today."

"Okay, I'm listening. Get it over with."

Julie looked around to make sure the cats weren't within earshot and read the first transcript.

**February 4  9:20 a.m.**

O: "No offense, *amigo*, but did you groom yourself today?"

W: "Why?"

O: "I was just noticing your fur doesn't look quite as shiny and smooth as it usually does."

W: "I decided to take today off."

O: "How come?"

W: "I've been grooming for like a hundred days in a row and just felt like I needed a day off."

O: "I get it. Everyone needs a break. So I'm curious if when you groom, do you have a routine you consistently follow?"

**W:** "Yeah, I start with my rear end to get it over with. Then I do my tail, back paws, back legs, front legs, and then back and stomach. Always in that order. How 'bout you?"

**O:** "I do my stomach first. Then back legs, paws, rear, back, tail, and finally my front legs and paws."

**W:** "Do you ever get lost? Say your mind wanders and you forget where you are in the process?"

**O:** "Yeah, all the time. I'll start thinking about the chipmunk I saw earlier in the backyard and I'll realize I've already groomed my stomach, and here I am grooming it again. I'll feel like an idiot."

**W:** "Ha. The same thing happens to me. After thousands of times, you can still lose track of what you're doing."

**O:** "Grooming ain't brain surgery, but it does require a bit of focus."


Darryl said, "That's funny that Wendell is too lazy to groom himself."

"Speaking of grooming one's self, when was the last time you took a shower?"

"I don't know. I don't keep track of those things. I'm sure it was within the last few weeks. Hey, you're changing the subject! We're supposed to be analyzing the cats' conversations."

"Sorry, but when you said, 'too lazy to groom himself' I immediately thought of you."

"Well, I'm glad you're thinking of me, honey, but I'm probably not lazier than Wendell."

"That's debatable. Wendell might be lazy about grooming but not exercise. Listen to this conversation."


**February 4  1:31 p.m.**

**O:** "I saw you going hog wild on the scratching post earlier."

**W:** "It was a good workout. I did almost ten minutes straight. I was in the zone."

**O:** "Impressive. What did you think about when you were scratching away?"

**W:** "I imagined I was clawing Baldy's head."

**O:** "Ha. I'll have to try that."

**W:** "You'd be amazed how much more energy you can summon when you pretend you're shredding either Baldy or Shorty.

96

**O:** "Speaking of B and S, what if we put their feet in a tub of quick-dry cement?"

**W:** "Oh, *amigo*, you watch too many gangster movies."

Julie said, "Even though they haven't hatched a sensible plan to kill us yet, they're still actively scheming. That scares me. Maybe I should call Patricia Van Winkle."

"That animal-psychic scam artist? No way."

"Listen, she was obviously right about the cats hating us."

Darryl shook his head. "She probably says the same thing to all the cat owners. That way her clients will freak out and keep paying for her scam service."

"She could get information to save our lives."

"We all have to die sometime."

"Do you really want your obituary to say: 'Darryl Belcher was murdered by his two little kitty cats.'?"

"Why not? That could be my claim to fame. I might even have my own Wikipedia page."

## Chapter 35

The next day Julie marched into the family room. "Darryl, what the heck? Why are the cats wearing bells?"

"So we hear them if they sneak up on us. Also, if they somehow get into our bedroom at night, the bells will wake us up. It's the perfect solution to prevent a surprise attack. You're welcome."

"Every time the cats move, the constant noise will drive us nuts!"

"It might be annoying at first, but we'll get used to it, and eventually we won't hear them at all. We'll just tune them out."

"But that defeats the purpose of them wearing bells, genius. If we just ignore them, it makes no sense."

"Oh, I see what you're saying. Hmm. Let's try it for a day and see how it goes."

Julie groaned. "Okay, here are today's conversations."

**February 5  10:17 a.m.**

O: "Here's an idea. We drop something heavy on them, like a piano."

W: "*Amigo*, have you been sniffing the dope today? How would we even pull that off? Besides, there's no piano in the house."

O: "I said, 'like a piano.' There must be something big and heavy we can drop on them."

W: "Hmm... You just gave me an idea."

O: "What?"

**W:** I'm pretty sure it will work, but let me think about it awhile. We can discuss it later."

**O:** "Can you give me a hint?"

**W:** "It might be messy, but it would smash B and S to smithereens."

Darryl said, "Holy crap. What does he have in mind?"

"I have no idea, but Wendell has clearly come up with a gruesome way to kill us."

"At least it sounds like a quick death. Read the next transcript to see if he reveals more about his idea."

"No, it's not really relevant."

Catching Julie by surprise, Darryl reached out, grabbed the transcript from her hand, and read it out loud.

### February 5   11:06 a.m.

**W:** "*From Russia with Love* was on last night."

**O:** "The old Bond flick?"

**W:** "No, dummy. I'm talking about Blondie and Ivan the Terrible."

**O:** "Oh, yeah. I heard him come in but kept my distance."

**W:** "I hate that guy."

**O:** "Me too. He's so mean, and scary looking. He actually makes Dagwood look good."

**W:** "Let's not exaggerate. Nobody makes Dagwood look good."

**O:** "I don't know. I'm used to Dagwood. Ivan is an unpredictable threat."

**W:** "If only there was a way to neutralize him."

**O:** "Maybe we should add him to the list of people we bump off."

**W:** "I wish I could, but the plan I came up with doesn't account for eliminating Ivan."

**O:** "Maybe we can off him later?"

**W:** "Please stop using 'off' as a verb. You're not in the Mafia. You're not even Italian."

**O:** "How 'bout this? I'll make Ivan an offer he can't refuse."

**W:** "Ugh. Don't take this personally, but I'm going somewhere else now."

Darryl said, "This is at least the third time they've brought up Ivan the Terrible. Tell me the truth: Is there something going on between you two?"

"No. No. No. It's not what you think." *Crap. He knows something's going on.*

"What then?"

"I don't know where they came up with that. Again they watch a lot of TV, and they seem to have vivid imaginations. Maybe there was some show that mentioned Ivan the Terrible."

"We'll get back to that. Read the last conversation."

**February 5  1:53 p.m.**

**O:** "WTF? I was snoozing peacefully on the couch. When I woke up, I was wearing this stupid bell."

**W:** "Welcome to bell hell, *amigo*. I was awake and struggled, but Dagwood still managed to get one on me."

**O:** "What are we, friggin' cows?"

**W:** "It seems like a violation of our civil rights."

**O:** "Could it be a cruel joke? Is this April Fools' Day?"

**W:** "No, that's still two months away. I can't imagine why he did it, unless Dagwood has a new obsession with bells."

**O:** "We always knew he was a ding-a-ling. It's just one more reason to fly the coop."

**W:** "Yeah. I'm glad we finally settled on a plan to eliminate the dastardly duo."

**O:** "It certainly sounds like it will work."

**W:** "I don't see how it can fail."

**O:** "When will we do it?"

**W:** "Let's do it Friday night after Blondie and Dagwood have gone to bed. That will give us the weekend to assess any fallout."

**O:** "Great. I'm counting the hours till it's finally done."

**W:** "You and me both, *amigo*."

Darryl said, "Oh my god! They've come up with a plan to kill us, and we somehow missed it."

"Well at least we know *when* they plan to do it, this Friday. And if it's Wendell's plan, we know it involves smashing us to smithereens."

"But how do we stop them?"

"I could get Patricia Van Winkle to find out what the cats are up to."

"All right. But get her to come down on her price."

"I'll try. And Darryl, take the bells off the cats. It's just making them even more pissed at us. If you remove the bells today, maybe there's a chance they'll forgive us."

"All right, but it's your funeral. And more importantly, mine too."

## Chapter 36

Julie called Linda after her shift at Supercuts ended. "You want to hear something funny? Darryl thinks I'm having an affair."

"You're not, are you?" *I wouldn't blame you.*

"No! He just thinks I am."

"Why?"

"It has to do with those cat conversations. Rick has come over a few times when Darryl was out."

"That's not good. They hate each other. Aren't you worried about them crossing paths?"

"Not too much. I know when Darryl goes to the casino he'll be gone for several hours, and Rick's never here too long."

"Okay, so why does Darryl think you're having an affair?"

"You know that Rick has a role in *Fiddler on the Roof*. So he stays in character most of the time with a Russian accent. He even talks to the cats in a menacing way with his accent."

"And the cats think he's a real Bolshevik?"

"I guess so. Anyway, after Rick leaves, the cats often talk about 'the Russian, Ivan the Terrible' in a frightened and disparaging way.'"

Linda laughed. "That's hilarious. Rick didn't tell me he was terrorizing your cats!"

"And hearing these conversations from the transcripts, Darryl has put two and two together and come up with five. He thinks I'm having an affair with some Russian dude."

"Aren't you going to tell Darryl that it's your brother and not some Communist lover?"

Julie shook her head. "I thought about it, but decided not to. Darryl doesn't like Rick, so he would be mad if he knew he was over here."

"Why does he dislike Rick so much?"

"I think because he mocked Darryl for wanting to be a professional gambler. Rick kept calling him 'Kenny,' as in Kenny Rogers. That infuriated Darryl. And Darryl mocks Rick for wanting to be an actor, so the animosity is mutual."

"I get it. But in the meantime, Darryl thinks you're having an affair."

"That's fine with me. Let him think that. It will drive him crazy. Chances are he's having an affair with a Hispanic floozy, so turnabout is fair play."

"You really have a great marriage, don't you?"

"Don't get me started."

## Chapter 37

Julie walked into the bedroom and saw Darryl texting on the bed. "Are you ready for today's cat conversation? Again, it's pretty ominous."

"I'm guessing they still haven't revealed how they plan to kill us on Friday."

"Not a clue."

"What did they say?"

"First there's another message from Elon."

## Message From Elon Musk, CEO of Cat Chat

I hope your week is going better than mine. Yesterday my self-driving Tesla decided to drive itself into a brick wall. Don't tell the stockholders. LOL. So how is

Cat Chat working out for you? If you're like most newbies, you're having a ton of fun eavesdropping on your cats' telepathic conversations. Over the last few weeks, you've undoubtedly discovered fascinating facts about your cats' likes, dislikes, and desires. Just the other day, I learned that Morpheus and Capricorn-X enjoyed a lively debate about the gravitational force of the newly discovered black hole in the galaxy. My cats never cease to amaze me, just as I'm sure yours have amazed you too! Remember, your free membership expires soon, but you're invited to renew for another eleven months for a mere $399. In addition to Cat Chat, you can have a FREE 30-day trial of any of our newest brainwave-translation apps: Doggy Dialogue, Bird Banter, Turtle Talk, Chicken Chatter, and Goldfish Gab. All are brand new and ready for you to download so you can learn more about your other pets. Maybe someday I'll develop brainwave-analysis software that will reveal what women are really thinking. And I'll charge a fortune! LOL. Elon

Darryl said, "When he comes up with it, I'd pay good money for the women's brainwave app."

"Really? I don't think you'd *want* to know my thoughts most of the time."

Darryl caught Julie's glare. "Perhaps not."

Julie grunted and read the transcript.

**February 6  3:24 p.m.**

**W:** "Are you excited? We're only a few days away from doing it."

**O:** "Yeah, I'm excited. I still have a few doubts though."

**W:** "Like what?"

**O:** "You know, potential collateral damage."

**W:** "You mean Hairdo?"

**O:** "Yep, plus Smarty Pants and Pacifier. They could be innocent victims."

**W:** "It's too bad, but there's no turning back. The die is cast. And some of the cast may die."

**O:** "I suppose so."

**W:** "Think positive. We'll permanently be rid of Baldy and Shorty. Imagine how great that'll feel."

O: "Pretty damn good."

W: "Independence day."

O: "Have you given any more thought about whether we'll stay together after we eliminate them?"

W: "Oh, *amigo*, we were having a nice conversation. Let's not spoil it."


"Darryl, what do you think they mean by 'some of the cast may die'?"

"No friggin' idea. These cats are nuts. What about what we talked about yesterday? See if you can lowball the psychic; get her to cut to the chase and find out what Little Hitler and Mussolini have in mind."

"So *now* you believe in psychics?"

Darryl put down his phone and looked at Julie. "No, I just think we're out of options."

"All right, I'll call Patricia tomorrow. Maybe she'll feel generous and drop her price. Who do you think Hairdo, Smarty Pants, and Pacifier are?"

"My guess is members of your clan. Hairdo could be Linda. Smarty Pants is probably your brother, Rick. And Pacifier is your mom because she always tries to make peace in the family."

"But why would they be collateral damage? They rarely come over. Their lives shouldn't be in danger."

"You got me. That's another question for the psychic. See if she'll take a few extra questions for no charge."

"Why would she?"

"Tell her I'll teach her how to play poker as a trade for her service.'"

Julie rolled her eyes. *Great idea. In the meantime, who's going to teach you?*

106

## Chapter 38

Darryl called Rowdy right after Julie left for work. "Rowdy, I feel like the world is closing in on me."

"What do you mean?" *When did I become his therapist?*

"Same old stuff, only worse. I'm more convinced than ever that Julie is having an affair. The cats keep mentioning some Russian who stops by when I'm out at night."

"And Julie still denies it?"

"Yep."

"Did you leave out a bottle of vodka, like I suggested?"

"Yeah, but it was inconclusive. I ended up drinking most of it, so I'm not sure if the Russian had any or not."

"Too bad. What else has you down?"

"I've blown through all my lottery winnings."

Rowdy's eyes widened. "What? You've spent the entire $50,000 from your first-year payout?"

"Yep. And then some. I've even tapped our credit cards for another $20,000."

"Wow. That's some serious gambling." *And losing.*

"I just can't believe how unlucky I've been. Last night I tried drawing to an inside straight six times and didn't hit even one."

"Everyone knows drawing to an inside straight is a long shot, Darryl."

"I know, but I would've won so much money."

"I'm sorry to hear the gambling profession hasn't panned out. Does Julie know you've gambled away all your money?"

"No, of course not. And I plan to hold off telling her as long as I can. Maybe there's still a chance I can win it back."

"Yeah, there's still a chance." *Fat chance.*

"Thanks, but that's not why I called. You know, the cats are still scheming to kill me."

"Are you sure that's what's going on? Again, it sounds a little crazy." *Crap, I'll never get off the phone.*

"There is absolutely no doubt in my mind. They are going to try to 'off' me Friday night."

"Why don't you just take them back to the shelter? Or drive them far away and drop them off."

"I know! That's the logical thing to do, but Julie won't hear of it. Even though the clock is ticking on our execution, she thinks we can miraculously get these two evil creatures to like us. But it will never happen."

"Huh. That's too bad, man." *Here's my chance to hang up.*

"I wanted to let you know, Rowdy, that if the worst happens and the cats succeed with their plans, you're in my will."

"You've blown through all your money. What's left in your will?"

"Not much, but a few nice things would go your way."

"Like what?"

"I've got a Michael Jordan autographed football that will be yours."

"He signed a *football*?"

"It's not *that* Michael Jordan. It's a different guy, but same name. He played lineman for the Bears back in the '90s."

"Oh, all right."

"I also have a nice trophy I got for winning the chugging contest at Clancy's in 2015. I'm not sure what it's worth, but it's decorative and you could put it on your mantle. If I am murdered by the cats, the trophy is yours, buddy."

"Wow, I don't know what to say." *Yes I do. Take me out of your stupid will.*

"I also have an old rowing machine I haven't used for years. It doesn't work, and it's a little rusty, but I'm sure you could figure out how to fix it."

"Well, thanks, Darryl. But you *really* don't have to leave me anything in your will. I mean *really*, you don't." *Can the dude take a hint?*

"No, I insist."

"I just pray the cats don't kill you."

"Thanks, Rowdy."

## Chapter 39

Julie walked into the family room and said, "Here's today's only conversation."

Darryl sat up on the couch and opened a bag of Fritos. "How many days left of free translations?"

"We have one more day unless we decide to pay for the year's membership."

"I'm glad it's almost over. These conversations are boring me."

"You're kidding? The fact they plan to kill us is boring you?"

"I admit that part is a bit unnerving. I guess I'm tired of all their putdowns, calling me smelly, stupid, and a slacker. Where do they get off criticizing me?"

"I do it all the time."

"Yeah, but I tune you out. You're like white noise."

Julie pouted. "Well, try to pay attention now."

**February 7   4:19 p.m.**

**O:** "What day is it?"

**W:** "Wednesday."

**O:** "That's funny. I keep thinking it's Thursday."

**W:** "I wish it were Thursday. Then we'd be only one day away from exterminating Tweedle Dee and Tweedle Dumbass."

O: "I can't wait."

W: "You know when the deed is done Friday night, we will be the most obvious suspects."

O: "When this is over, we should get the hell out of Springfield as quickly as possible. Otherwise we could face a lot of heat."

W: "I'm not so sure, Chief Blue Belly is too incompetent to pin this on us."

As he pulled out a handful of chips, Darryl said, "Why do they keep mentioning Springfield? And who the heck is Chief Blue Belly?"

"I have no idea. I left a message with Patricia Van Winkle. Hopefully, I'll talk with her tomorrow."

"That's cutting it close. If you don't connect with her tomorrow, maybe we should spend Friday night at your sister's."

"I agree. I'll call Patricia again and leave a message that it's urgent."

"Remember to ask her if she'll give us a few extra questions for free poker lessons. She doesn't have to know my track record. Just tell her I'm a professional gambler."

"Darryl, she's a psychic. She can read minds. She'll know it's a crappy offer." Julie noticed Darryl's downcast face. "All right, I'll try."

## Chapter 40

Thursday morning, on her first break at Supercuts, Julie called Patricia from her car. "Hello, Patricia. It's Julie Belcher. I have a time-critical job for you."

"What is it, Julie?"

"Can you communicate with my cats and find out the answers to a few questions?"

Patricia lit a cigarette. "How many questions do you want answered?"

"I have a total of eight questions."

"Okay, the answers will cost you $20 a piece, for a total of $160."

Julie exhaled. "Here's the thing, Darryl is giving me a hard time about the cost. Could you do it for a bit less? We're a little short on funds, and our lives may be in danger."

"Eight questions are $160. Sorry."

"Darryl said if you give us a few freebies, he'll teach you how to play poker."

Growing irritated, Patricia said, "Eight questions are still $160. And I can tell from your voice that you think the poker offer stinks."

"You're right, it does. Put the $160 on the same credit card I used before."

"I'll do that. Now what are your questions?"

"Last time we talked, you said that Oliver and Wendell hate us. Well, you were right. In fact, they more than hate us; we think they're plotting to kill us."

Patricia chuckled. "What? Are you pulling my leg?"

"No, I'm not. This is serious. They're going to try to kill us tomorrow night."

"Julie, are you taking drugs?" *Another crackpot client. That's three this week.*

"No, I never do drugs. Well, at least not in the last few days. Listen, Patricia, our cats have been plotting to murder us for weeks now."

"How do you know that?" *Maybe this is a prank.*

"It's not important how we know. The fact is they plan to kill us sometime tomorrow night in our house. So you can understand why it's so important to get some answers right away."

Patricia grimaced. "I can try to communicate with your cats tomorrow, but I'm on a very tight schedule. You haven't given me much notice."

"Please try. It's obviously extremely important. It could be a matter of life and death."

"Are you sure you're not imagining this?" *This must be a hoax.*

"No, I'm not. You can determine that yourself by confirming it with Oliver and Wendell."

"Okay, but it sounds ridiculous. What are your questions?"

"The first questions is: 'How do they plan to kill us?'"

"You don't know how?"

"If we did, it would be a lot easier to prevent it."

Patricia made some notes. "All right. What are the other questions?"

"Who is Chiquita Bonita? What is her relationship with Darryl? Who is Hairdo? Who is Smarty Pants? Who is Pacifier? Who is Chief Blue Belly?"

Patricia took a minute to jot down all of Julie's questions. "Julie, have you had any recent head injuries, like a concussion or any hard blow to the noggin?"

"No, definitely not. Trust me, although I'm extremely stressed, I'm still thinking clearly."

"All right. By my count, that's seven questions. Do you have one more?"

"Why do the cats keep mentioning Springfield?"

"I've written all of them down. I'll try to get answers to you by tomorrow. If not, by Monday."

"No. No. No. Monday will be too late. We might be dead by then. Please try to have answers by tomorrow."

"I'll see what I can do. Julie, just out of curiosity, is there any mental illness in your family?"

"Not that I'm aware of, but ever since I married Darryl, I get asked that a lot."

## Chapter 41

Early on Thursday afternoon, after losing $1,473 playing blackjack online, Darryl called Patricia. "Hello, Patricia. It's Darryl Belcher."

"Who?"

"Darryl Belcher, Julie's husband. You know, we're the couple with the two cats, Oliver and Wendell."

"Oh, yes. Hello, Darryl. What can I do for you?"

"Did Julie give you her questions for the cats?"

"Yes, she did. I spoke with her this morning."

Darryl took a swig of beer. "Good. In addition to Julie's questions, I have a few of my own."

"Okay." *I hope his questions aren't as nutty as his wife's.*

"But I have to make something clear. It's important that you *not* tell Julie I called and gave you more questions."

"I won't. My clients' confidentiality is very important to me."

"Good. So how much do you charge?"

"My standard fee is $20 per question."

"Here's the thing, Patricia, we're tight on money right now, and you would be doing me a huge favor by getting just a few easy answers from the cats."

"My standard fee is $20 per question." *Here we go again.*

"You could potentially save our lives."

"It's still $20 per question."

"I don't know if Julie mentioned it, but I'm a full-time professional gambler. And all modesty aside, I've been quite successful. In fact, I won a million dollars last year."

"Good for you." *Yet you have no money?* "What's your point, Darryl?"

"I'll make you a great offer. If you don't charge me for your service, I'll teach you how to play poker. With one lesson from me, you could be the best player in your poker league."

"I'm not in a poker league, and I have no interest in learning."

"You could start your own poker league of animal communicators. With my coaching, you could be the best player among your psycho friends."

"I think you mean *psychic* friends. And it's still $20 per question." *This guy is getting on my nerves.*

"Okay, Patricia, it's your loss."

"I'll find a way to live with it. What are your questions?"

"The first one is: 'Who is the Russian?' In other words, what is his relationship with Julie?"

Patricia jotted down the question. "All right, but the cats may not know exactly who he is."

"I understand, but ask them anyway. And ask if the Russian and Julie ever showed physical affection in front of them. Like did they hold hands or kiss? Or any other type of affection?"

"Really, Darryl? All right, I'll find out." *What a marriage.*

"Ask them if Julie's had other men in the house while I've been gone. And find out who they are."

Patricia made notes. "Okay. I'll try my best to find out."

"As Julie may have told you, the cats are plotting to kill both of us."

"She did tell me. I find that extremely hard to believe, but I'll see what I can find out."

"There's no doubt about it. They are plotting to kill us. So ask them if they'd be willing to make a deal with me."

"What type of deal?"

"Whether or not they'd be willing to spare us if I make some big changes. For example, I promise I won't yell at them anymore or swat them with magazines. Plus, I'll start showering regularly. And if they really do want to be outdoor cats, I'll let them go outside to their heart's content."

"All right." Patricia wrote: *Batshit crazy*.

"Finally, I'd be willing to pay you $100 if you would fudge some of the answers you give to Julie."

"Like what?"

"She probably asked you to find out who Chiquita Bonita is."

"I'm not going to reveal what questions she asked. Again, that's confidential."

"Well, let's just say, hypothetically, if she *did* ask about Chiquita Bonita, just tell her the cats said there's no such person, and they just made it up."

"I'm sorry, but I can't do that. I'm going to get truthful answers to Julie's questions, just as I'm going to get truthful answers to your questions. I'm not going to 'fudge' the answers, as you put it."

"Let's make it $200."

Glancing at the time, Patricia said, "No, Darryl. Listen, I've got to go. Give me a couple of days, and I'll have answers to your questions. I can charge it to the same credit card Julie used."

"No, a couple of days might be too long. These cats could be eating our dead bodies by then."

"Darryl, Julie told me you've worked in construction. Were you ever conked in the head with something hard and heavy, like a steel beam, concrete block, or a railroad tie?

"All of the above. Why?"

"Just curious." *Figures*.

## Chapter 42

Julie carried the two transcripts into the bedroom. "Okay, Darryl, here are the only two transcripts from today, our last free day. They didn't say how they plan to do it, but they did reveal when."

"So we can't record them anymore?"

"Nope. This is it, unless we want to shell out $400 for a year's membership."

"I suppose if they're going to kill us tomorrow, there's no need to see anymore conversations. What did they say?"

Julie read the first transcript.

**February 8   10:43 a.m.**

**O:** "Are you excited, *amigo*?"

**W:** "Super excited. I was so pumped up, I couldn't sleep more than fifteen hours yesterday."

O: "Me either."

W: "So are you ready to pull the plug on Baldy and Shorty?"

O: "As ready as I'll ever be. What time will we do it?"

W: "Tomorrow night at ten o'clock."

O: "Okay, then. Let's synchronize our watches."

W: "Just one problem, Mr. Bond. We don't wear watches."

O: "That gives me an idea. Let's give ourselves code names. You can call me 007."

W: "Sure. It will be great to carry out this mission with you, 007."

O: "Thank you. What should I call you?"

W: "Call me the Terminator."

O: "Ooh, I like that better than mine. Forget 007. Instead call me Terminator 2."

W: "You're friggin' kidding me? You can't change your code name on a whim because you like mine better."

O: "Our code names aren't carved in stone. I can change mine if I want to."

W: "But you're just copying mine."

O: "Frankly, I don't see the problem. You're the Terminator, and I'm Terminator 2. They're different names."

W: "No. It's just too confusing if we're both Terminators."

O: "I think you're just being abstinent."

W: "I think you mean 'obstinate.' Let me make this clear: There can only be one Terminator."

O: "I disagree."

W: "I'm the Terminator, and I'm terminating this discussion."

"There you go, Julie. They're planning to terminate us at 10:00 p.m. tomorrow."

"Terminate us. Pull the plug. Eliminate us. Off us. They have more euphemisms for our deaths. What's next – 'Baldy and Shorty will be pushing up daisies'?"

"So we stay at your sister's tomorrow night?"

"Right. We should be safe for tonight, though, if we keep the lights on, lock the bedroom door, and push the dresser against it. Here's the second conversation."

**February 8  11:27 a.m.**

**O:** "Okay, you win. You can be the one and only Terminator."

**W:** "Good. I'm glad we've settled that matter. Are you okay with being 007?"

**O:** "Yes, it's fine. I like that 007 has a 'license to kill.'"

**W:** "You do understand that just because the fictional 007 has a 'license to kill' doesn't mean you'll be granted immunity if we get caught?"

**O:** "Of course, but it's kind of fun to pretend."

**W:** "Look, 007, our mission is not fun and games. What we're doing tomorrow night is serious business with potentially serious consequences."

**O:** "Understood. Don't worry, Terminator, I won't let you down."

**W:** "All right, 007, I will rendezvous with you tomorrow at the appointed time and place to carry out the plan. Until then, let's keep a low profile."


Julie said, "That's it. We still have no clues about how they're going to kill us."

"They've obviously come up with a scheme they think will work. This is very troubling."

"Well, look at it this way, after tomorrow night, it will be over one way or another."

## Chapter 43

Darryl sat on the edge of the bed and said, "So Patricia Van Stinkle never called back, huh?"

"Van *Winkle*, and no, I've left two messages that we urgently need to know what she found out."

"If she can't get you answers today, it's too late. It's almost 9:45 p.m. The cats are going to make their play soon. You might as well cancel with her."

"I suppose you're right."

"We should probably think about heading over to your sister's too."

At 9:55 p.m. sharp, Julie and Darryl put on their coats. Julie said, "Wait. Before we leave, I still need to call Patricia to cancel. Why is the TV in the family room still on?"

"To keep the cats occupied."

"It's silly to leave the TV on all night. Why don't you turn it off?" Julie walked into the bathroom, shut the door, and called the animal communicator. "Hello, Patricia. I'm surprised to catch you in. We've been waiting for your answers. I was ready to cancel."

"I'm sorry, Julie. I've been super busy. I have a desperate client with a Saint Bernard that thinks he can fly. He keeps trying to jump off their balcony. Anyway, I was just about to call you."

Julie asked, "What did you find out?" and then held her breath.

"First, I have some good news. The cats are *not* planning to kill you."

"Really? So they called off their plan?" *Thank God.*

"Well not exactly; they never planned to kill either of you. In fact, they had no idea what I was talking about."

"Are you sure they weren't just being guarded? I mean, they might not trust you."

"No, I could tell they were candid. I don't know how you came up with this notion that the cats had been contemplating your murder, but they did mention a plan to terminate Baldy and Shorty."

"I don't understand. Aren't we Baldy and Shorty? Patricia, hold on. I just heard a loud crash. Let me call you right back." Julie hurried out of the bathroom and into the family room. "Oh my god! Darryl, what the hell happened to the TV?"

"This is so bizarre. If I hadn't seen it with my own eyes, I wouldn't have believed it. As I walked into the family room, both cats were on top of the TV with their front paws against the wall and their back paws on the TV. They pushed with their hind legs and toppled the set onto the floor. It was like they had practiced the maneuver."

Julie waved her arms. "Why didn't you stop them?"

"I didn't have time. They pushed the TV over the moment I walked into the family room. The set is probably broken beyond repair. I hate those stupid cats."

"What was on the TV when they pushed it over?"

*The Simpsons.* Why?"

"Do you remember exactly what was on the screen when it happened?"

"I think Homer was yelling at Bart."

As Julie stared at the shattered TV, she said, "Baldy and Shorty."

"What?"

"The yellow duo." *Of course.*

"Huh?"

"Nothing. I need to call Patricia back." Julie went back into the bathroom and redialed the number. "Hello, Patricia. Sorry about that. Where were we?"

"I was telling you the cats plan to terminate Baldy and Shorty."

"Okay, I think they just did. Long story, but do you have answers to my other questions?"

"Yes. Hairdo is Baldy's wife, Smarty Pants is Shorty's sister, and Pacifier is the baby in the family."

"Marge, Lisa, and Maggie. Okay, what else did you find out?"

"Chief Blue Belly is the police chief. Finally, the cats think they live in a town called Springfield. I hope this makes more sense to you than it does to me."

Julie nodded. "Yes, it all makes sense now. The cats never intended to kill us, which is all that matters. Did you learn the identity of Chiquita Bonita?"

"Yes, she's Darryl's female friend, Maya."

"Ugh. I knew he was having an affair." *If the cats won't kill him, I will.*

"I'm very sorry, Julie."

"How many times has she been over to our house?"

"About a dozen times. Of course, always when you're at work."

"I'm not sure I want to know, but did the cats say if she and Darryl were affectionate?"

Patricia paused before answering. "It sounds like it. They indicated Darryl always hugs her when she comes over. Also, she's sat on Darryl's lap a few times. Oh, and Darryl always kisses her when she leaves."

Julie felt numb. "Huh. I don't know whether to be ecstatic the cats aren't planning to kill me or furious at Darryl for cheating on me. Or both. This is a lot to absorb."

Julie walked back to the foyer where Darryl was standing waiting to leave. She looked him in the eyes. "Do you want the good news or the bad news first?"

"The good news, of course."

"She said the cats are not planning to kill us."

"That's fantastic, but what about all that talk about offing Baldy and Shorty?"

"They wanted to turn off *The Simpsons*, meaning Homer and Bart, aka Baldy and Shorty. That's why they just destroyed our TV."

"Wow. That's wild. And we thought they were talking about us. What a relief." After sitting, Darryl exhaled. "Okay, what's the bad news?"

"First I want to clear the air and make a confession. The Russian the cats talked about was Rick."

"Your *brother* Rick?"

"Yes, he's in *Fiddler on the Roof* and plays a Bolshevik, so he likes to stay in character."

"Why didn't you just tell me, instead of allowing me to think you were having an affair?"

"Well, I know how much you dislike Rick, and I was sure you wouldn't be happy to know he was coming over here a lot."

"Yeah, that's true. Even though I'm not happy, I'm glad I wasn't home when he slithered over to see you."

Julie took a deep breath. "So, Darryl, do you have anything to confess? Maybe you can explain Chiquita Bonita. And don't lie, because Patricia told me everything."

"So you know about Maya?"

"Yes."

"I'm so sorry. I should've told you."

Julie tried to subdue her simmering anger. "I'm listening. What's your lame excuse for being with this girl?"

"I love her."

"You *love* her?" *Oh no.*

"She's been a big part of my life for the last ten years, and it was important for us to stay connected."

"Ten years?" *It's worse than I'd imagined.*

"Yeah, I assume Patricia also told you about Nicole."

"Nicole? Is that another girlfriend?"

"No, she's my wife."

"*I'm* your wife. What are you talking about?" *Is this the 'Twilight Zone'?*

"Before you, I married Nicole."

"Whoa. I'm confused. You never mentioned being married to a woman named Nicole. Why not?"

"Because she's Maya's mother, and I hadn't told you about her yet."

Julie gasped. "You're having an affair with your ex-wife's daughter?"

"No, Maya is my daughter too. She's ten years old."

"You have a daughter? Nicole's daughter?"

"Yes."

"When did your marriage with Nicole end?"

"Hmm. That's a good question."

"Darryl, when did your marriage end?"

"Well, here's the thing, it never did end. We're still married on paper. We talked about filing for divorce but just never got around to it."

"What? So you married me while you were still married to another woman with whom you have a ten-year-old daughter?"

"All true. Pretty crazy, huh?"

Julie exhaled. "Is there any vodka left? I need a stiff drink." *Or ten.*

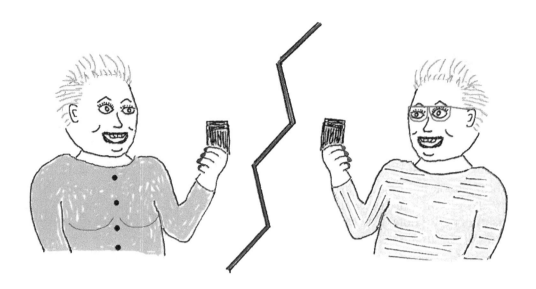

## Chapter 44

*One month later*

After uploading her photo to Tinder, Julie called Linda. "Congratulate me. The marriage is annulled. Darryl is gone. I'm on Tinder and am back in the game."

"Good for you. I'm sure you'll have fun being single."

"I hope so, but it will be a little weird dating again."

"It's like riding a bicycle."

"Yeah, blindfolded into heavy traffic."

"Has Darryl gotten all of his stuff out of the house?"

Julie smiled. "Yep, every last piece of crap he owned. He's completely moved back in with Nicole. He's her pain in the ass now."

"And he took Wendell and Oliver with him?"

"Amazing, right? After all we've been through, you wouldn't think he'd want anything to do with them. But Maya adores the cats, and it seems to be mutual."

"And Nicole?"

"According to Darryl, she doesn't like cats, but Maya made such a fuss that Nicole agreed to a trial basis. Also they're avoiding watching *The Simpsons* at all costs."

"Any idea why the cats hated Homer and Bart so much?"

"Yes, I had Patricia find out. They thought 'Baldy' and 'Shorty' were cruel to their cat, Snowball, especially when they put her in the dishwasher."

Linda laughed. "Sounds like something Darryl would do."

"Yep, sometimes I think Darryl and Homer are twins separated at birth."

"You could check on Ancestrry.com."

"I'd likely find out that Darryl was only a generation or two removed from Neanderthals. Anyway I won't miss him, but I will miss Max."

"What happened to him?"

"With Darryl gone, I can't afford to rent this house on my Supercuts take-home pay, so I'm moving to an apartment. I found a new home for Max with a family and a big fenced yard. Best of all: no cats to torment him."

"Good for Max. Does Darryl still owe you money?"

Julie shook her head. "No, believe it or not, he's all paid up. Last week he won over $27,000 at some poker tournament in Atlantic City. Although he's still many thousands in the hole, this tournament bolstered his confidence to keep going with his ridiculous dream of being a professional gambler."

"How do you feel about him now that you've had a chance to process everything? He married you when he was still married to Nicole, which is both slimy and illegal. Do you hate him?"

"No, I don't hate him. He's a big jerk, but I feel a bit sorry for him, and I feel especially sorry for Nicole."

"And how are you getting along with your new roommates?"

"The new cats? Fine. Chester and Charlie are good boys."

"Any bad vibes like you had with Wendell and Oliver?"

Julie glanced at her cats asleep on the couch. "Not at all; these cats are friendly, loving, and very sweet."

"That's a relief."

"But just to be safe, I've kept on with Cat Chat."

"Wow. You actually sprang for the $400?"

"I put it on Darryl's credit card. He doesn't know it yet, and I'm sure he'll go ballistic, but I figure he owes me for all the aggravation."

"And what have you learned from these cat conversations?"

"So far, just a few things. Chester thinks the water stain looks like Liberace. Whereas Charlie thinks it looks like Elton John."

"Cute. What else?"

"Chester's favorite color is chartreuse and Charlie's is mauve."

"Interesting. I thought cats were color-blind."

"I guess not. And Chester likes Barbra Streisand, but Charlie prefers Adele."

"I'm with Charlie on that one."

"Chester's favorite movie is *The Little Mermaid*, and Charlie's is *The Princess Bride*."

"Any mention of your perfume?"

Julie nodded. "They both love the fragrance. Chester called it 'exquisite' and Charlie said, 'it's simply divine.'"

"Great. So all is good with your fur babies?"

"Yeah, absolutely. Oh, just one thing. They said if I ever tried to bathe them again, they'd claw my face off."

\*\*\*\*\*

Later that day, Julie opened Tinder to see the three men who had selected her. She looked at photos of Earl, who had bloodshot eyes, Clem, who was missing a front tooth, and Zeke, who had a big tattoo of a scorpion on his neck. Julie swiped right on all three pictures. She smiled and thought: *I hope they like cats.*

## Worth Noting

This book would never have been written without the inspiration of my two tabbies, Pokey and Smokey, who were best friends and partners in crime.

Writing this book was also greatly helped by the suggestions and encouragement of my editor, and fellow cat owner, Jill Welsh.

If you enjoyed *Our Cats are Plotting to Kill Us*, my other books are listed on the next page. These previous books are more serious, thought-provoking, and educational. Just kidding. They're all quite silly.

Finally, while this book is still fresh in your mind, please go to Amazon and do a review. Even a few words would be appreciated.

Thanks for reading.

Jim Tilberry

# Other Books by Jim Tilberry

***Revenge of the Vegetarian*** is a humorous spin on vegetarianism and the meat-eating culture. This hilarious book makes fun of almost everyone who eats food from vegans to beef eaters, from dieters to overeaters.

***Coffee Dates from Hell*** is a wacky work of fiction that tells stories of hilariously awkward first dates, including coffee dates of Abraham Lincoln, Albert Einstein, J. Edgar Hoover and other famous people. Coffee dates also include a serial killer, cannibal, and Siamese twins.

**Mondays With Morty: Offbeat Lessons for $uccess** is a spoof of books on how to be successful, with Morty, an elderly mentor, sharing his misguided and convoluted wisdom with a young man. Morty's weekly lessons are often absurdly flawed and comically confusing.

***TRUMP DOG: A Wild Tale of Lies, Hair Dye, and Dog Poop*** takes place a few years in the future when people come to believe that Donald Trump was reincarnated as a dog. When the dog's owner attempts to cash in on his new fame, his life quickly spins out of control.

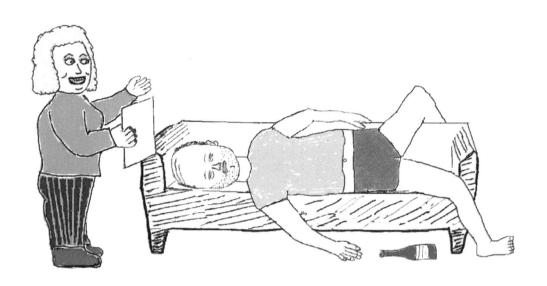

Made in the USA
Las Vegas, NV
11 December 2023